Juliana was herself a victim of domestic abuse that spanned a period of three decades, a subsequent survivor and now a warrior in the war against violence and abuse in all its forms. She is a retired Jungian based, Soul Centred Psychotherapist, whose wholistic practices were based on the premise that "The body Remembers". As a consequence of her own personal journey with abuse and her training and experience as a psychotherapist, she gained a deep insight into the anatomy of human behaviour and how one's upbringing combined with personal internal and external experiences in life impact on the development of the "human psyche".

This book is dedicated to all victims of abuse, those who have lost their lives, those who are currently in the fight for their survival and for those who have been able to find their freedom.

Juliana Vasiljevic

KINGDOM OF WOLVES – THE JOURNEY

A true story of survival
and courage

AUSTIN MACAULEY PUBLISHERS™

LONDON * CAMBRIDGE * NEW YORK * SHARJAH

A CIP catalogue record for this title is available from the British Library.

ISBN 9781035801312 (Paperback)
ISBN 9781035801336 (ePub e-book)
ISBN 9781035801329 (Audiobook)

www.austinmacauley.com

First Published 2023
Austin Macauley Publishers Ltd®
1 Canada Square
Canary Wharf
London
E14 5AA

To my mother Sylvia (1936–2015), my inspiration.

To my children and my family, thank you for your love and support.

To Mary Coughlan, you enriched my life and healed my soul and for that I shall be ever grateful.

To Sonia and Marie, I would like to express my deepest gratitude for your continued enthusiasm and faith in me and for finding the time in your busy lives to help with the revision of this book.

To my sister Mariana, Karen and Anna, thank you for your encouragement and unconditional love.

Table of Content

A true story of survival, courage and the soul's journey to freedom, reclamation, redemption, and wholeness of spirit.

"In All Chaos There is a Cosmos, In All Disorder a Secret Order"

Carl Gustav Jung

Introduction

I was a silent victim of domestic abuse perpetrated by my spouse that spanned a period of three decades, during which I was verbally, physically, emotionally and psychologically abused. I was held captive not only by my fear of my spouse and his retribution, but also by my low self-esteem, insecurities and fears. I was a young, innocent and naïve eighteen years old when I met my soon to be spouse. He was also eighteen years old at the time but with a vastly different ethical background and ideologies about life. I was reared in quite a conservative and sheltered background and so I was both, unprepared for and too inexperienced to understand what I was committing to when I entered into the relationship with my abuser. With this book I would like to take you on a journey through the psychological and emotional labyrinth of the minds of both myself the victim of abuse, and my husband the perpetrator of abuse. I am hoping to demystify any previously held misconceptions and preconceptions that are attached to victims of long-term abuse, by providing an intimate account of my personal journey with domestic abuse, my subsequent survival and how I overcame my deep-rooted fears and great adversity to achieve my ultimate goals of freedom, redemption, reclamation and wholeness of spirit.

It felt imperative that I remain secretive about my abuse while it was occurring, this was for good reason. I had never spoken about what was happening in my relationship until I felt safe enough to talk about it and to seek the help I needed. It was not until after my husband and I separated that those who were closest to me were told of my abusive relationship. They were extremely shocked and horrified to learn that I was abused and stunned to hear of the longevity and severity of the abuse that I had undergone. I hid my abuse well, they said they found it difficult to reconcile the person whom they knew, having experienced me personally as being the opposite in character, had been the victim of long-term abuse. They perceived me to be strong willed, an independent thinker, intelligent, spirited, positive minded, humorous and for the most part thought of me as happy. The thing is that I was all those things at times in my life, which I believe is likely due to my innate desire to overcome adversity and my beleaguered but persistent fighting spirit. However, despite my instinct for survival there is no denying that I was also a victim at the mercy of my inexperience and my abusers stronger will and experience.

I can understand how it may be difficult for a person who has never been bullied, threatened, been a witness to, or has ever been at the receiving end of violence and abuse in their life to truly appreciate the extent of the detrimental psychological and emotional impairment that violence or any form of abuse has on a human-being, particularly those who have endured long-term abuse. This is not to imply that those of you who have not been a victim cannot imagine how it would feel to be a victim, or that you cannot empathise with a victim, but it does imply that you do not wholly understand a victim and why they would tolerate ongoing abuse of any kind. I hope that by speaking about my journey with domestic abuse that I can shed light on the complexities of abusive relationships and how they are contrived. My intention is to provide a candid and comprehensive insight into the profiles of both the victim and the abuser through my personal experience and inform those who seek to comprehend the anomalies of victimhood and how easy it is to fall prey to a predator.

From the Beginning

Looking back, I cannot remember having thought about predators, abusers and violence in relation to myself or that it could ever occur in my life, other than experiencing some bullying during my teenage years at school. It was a foreign concept to me and so it never entered my mind that I could become a victim of domestic abuse. This happened to other people, people I didn't know and I had been given no reason to think otherwise. As a child born in the early nineteen sixties, I was brought up to believe in fairy-tales and was fed a steady diet of shows like I Love Lucy, Happy Days, Laverne and Shirley, Bewitched, The Brady Bunch and all things Disney with its' perpetual optimism and "happily ever after" always the theme. Exposure to the bigger world was limited to the family television set, the home phone, the radio, the library and school, there were no mobile phones or computers and therefore no internet or social media. I led a completely sheltered life and so the prospect of real violence or abuse ever occurring to me was inconceivable in my protected world and naïve psyche.

I was a product of a society that was struggling to emerge from its conservative, outdated and religiously motivated moral beliefs and practices, however from the mid nineteen sixties through to the mid to late nineteen seventies there was social, political and cultural upheaval in much of the western world. The youth of the day were challenging societies ideals and norms, heralding the emergence of the "counterculture" and "hippies" who believed in peace, love, freedom of speech and sexual liberation. Young women growing up through this cultural, social and sexual revolution struggled with old and new beliefs and ideals. The clash between the generations creating a divide between those staunch believers who held outmoded thinking and those who fought for and desired change. It seems that even with the advent of this seeming emancipating reformation, sexual abuse and family and domestic abuse still thrived, remaining a taboo subject for personal familial discussion and general public conversation.

However, despite the anti-establishment cultural phenomenon and the growth of the 'civil rights" and "women's rights" movements the majority of western society remained steeped in their traditional principles and beliefs, my parents included. I was brought up in an environment where women were still relegated into two categories you were either a "good girl" or a "bad girl". To be a "good girl" meant that a woman was required to remain a virgin until she was married and to make her home, husband and children her top priority, whose needs were to be placed above her own. She was to remain married and loyal to her husband despite discovering that her and her husband were not sexually, emotionally or intellectually compatible. Divorce was still frowned upon by the majority of society and so a wife would be expected to tolerate her husbands' abusive behaviour if he was that way inclined. Society considered a husband and father to be the head of the house and ruler of his kingdom and so much leeway was given to him by a society dominated by patriarchal rule. Women were able to and did receive a general and higher education equal to that of their male counterparts, however generally they were encouraged to learn how to entertain and to comport themselves with the proper social graces. Deportment, proprietary behaviour, home economics and the fundamental basics of sewing and cooking were a priority. Men were encouraged to reach their highest potential academically, artistically and physically, while women were discouraged from having any long-term career aspirations because they were expected to get married, have children and manage all things domestic and of course "not" become a threat in the employment arena by taking away future employment from her male counter-parts. I can remember my career aspirations as a teenager of teetering between wanting to be an Air-hostess (flight attendant), a secretary (assistant/clerk) or a hairdresser, even though I secretly harboured what would have then been considered a lofty dream, of becoming a veterinarian.

I was one of many growing up in a sheltered world and so you can imagine that many young girls like myself were markedly ignorant of the realities of violent and abusive behaviour and violent and abusive men. Domestic abuse as we are coming to understand and acknowledge today was never a priority to be discussed in a public forum or considered to be a significant enough societal issue at that time and was mostly ignored when I was growing up. I can remember my mother talking amongst her peers about a neighbours' abusive husband in hushed voices as if it was subject that had to be whispered about and kept secret. There were many in our society both male and female who took an attitude of minding their own business where their neighbours, friends and family relationships were concerned, particularly if a couple were married.

People in general had a kind of "turn the other cheek" attitude, they believed that by minding their own business meant that whatever happened in their own homes would not be open to external scrutiny. There was a general attitude of apathy towards domestic violence as well as a prevalence of sexism towards women and predominance of male chauvinistic attitudes. During this era the policing bodies and the judicial system also reflected a society that did not take domestic violence as seriously as it should have. Many perpetrators of abuse were not punished in a manner that acted as a deterrent in fact, they were quite often given a rap on the knuckles, or if alcohol was involved the offender was asked to sleep off his intoxication with a night in a holding cell.

I grew up in a family in which I was the middle child of five, and the oldest daughter to Slavic parents who immigrated to Australia in the early 1950's from what was then the former Yugoslavia. They both arrived on separate occasions and through mutual acquaintances had met and married a short time later. Our family for the most part led quite a nomadic lifestyle, we were constantly on the move, I can remember coming home from school and finding that our home had been packed up and we were told that we were moving with no prior warning that a move was imminent. We moved suburbs within cities as well as to different states, which meant new neighbourhoods and therefore into differing sub-cultures. My mother must have been an expert packer because within a week of moving to our new premises she would have set up our home as if we had been living there for some time. It seemed to me that for my parents, leaving their friends behind hadn't affected them in the least and if it did neither of them allowed it to show.

Now as we look back, some of my siblings and I hypothesised that perhaps given their Slavic heritage it was possible that my parents had some ancestral gypsy blood coursing through their veins that kept them wanting to travel, see new places, meet new people, and start new ventures. However, to be more realistic we suspect that may have only played a very small part in their constant roving, one of my brothers even going so far as to suggest that it was more likely that they were always on move to keep one step ahead of the sheriff. My father was a scallywag and a scrapper, he possessed a burning desire to succeed, was unflinchingly determined and the type of person who looked for and found opportunity wherever he went. He was not afraid to try his hand at anything and probably had as many successes as he did failures but it was not for a lack of trying. He was gregarious, confident, brazen and had a sense of humour, he had an excellent work ethic and so he worked hard, often juggling two and sometimes three jobs a week to pay the bills and put food on the table. However, he was also known to be grandiose in his desires, obstinate in the extreme, impulsive, short tempered, autocratic and he had a compulsive propensity to stretch the truth. He also possessed narcissistic tendencies and so was inclined to indulge his self-serving ego.

Despite coming from a poor farming background in Serbia he had big dreams and aspirations and I imagine that he saw the post war western world as a place that could make those dreams come true. At that time the former Yugoslavia was under a communist/socialist regime and so he was not permitted to leave, nor did he have the contacts or necessary funds to buy his way to freedom. He decided quite naively that he would escape via motor bike, clandestinely crossing over into Italy by avoiding the official border crossing, with the intention of making his way to a port and then catching a ship ride to a Western destination. However, regrettably he had the great misfortune of crossing paths with a militant Italian border patrol unit who shot him as he tried to outrun them in his attempt to escape, which resulted with him sustaining a wound that fractured his right hip. He was then taken to an Italian prison camp, having surgery that left him with a permanent limp and in which he was subsequently interned for about twelve months. While there, he learned to speak fluent Italian and some Russian and had made some life-long friends with other inmates of various nationalities. It was not long after the end of World War Two, the camp was being disbanded, and so as luck would have it, he along with the other inmates were fortuitously offered the choice to immigrate by ship to either America, Canada, or Australia. He chose Australia because he received word that there was a someone of Yugoslav descent living in the city of Melbourne offering him a sponsorship and a place to live. This was where he later met and married my mother and where both my elder brothers were born.

My mother had also undergone her own heroic journey from the former Yugoslavia. She like many of her teenage counterparts at that time, was struggling to come to terms with old and new ideals while emerging from the embers of World War Two, chafing at the strictures of a communist/fascist regime. She was born and raised in the beautiful historic city of Maribor, which lies along the Drava River near the Austrian border in the state of Slovenia. She was only sixteen years old when she and a girlfriend had quite idealistically decided to fulfil their dream to travel the world, their plan was simplistic in nature, a reflection of their innocence. They intended to swim across the narrowest point of the Drava River (a tributary of the Danube) and into the democratic republic of Austria. They had planned to meet at a designated spot on the banks of the river, this part of the river was reputed to be the shortest crossing point between Maribor and Austria, a well-known route to freedom used by many escapees before them. My mother arrived at the designated time to meet her girlfriend only to find that her girlfriend had brought along her boyfriend, someone my mother did not know existed prior to that day.

However, undaunted the three had decided that they were going to swim across one at a time, the boyfriend went first making his way across to the other side without incident. He was quickly followed by his girlfriend who did likewise, it was then my mother's turn, she eased her way in the water, with her belongings draped at her side slowly making her way across, she had nearly completed the crossing when she encountered difficulty. She had either overestimated her swimming prowess or underestimated the waters unpredictable temperament, struggling to hold onto her belongings and swim at the same time. She managed to make it close to the water's edge on the other side but found herself to exhausted to continue, she could remember thinking that she was going to drown. Fortunately for her, providence stepped in saving her from becoming the next victim to capitulate to the Drava Rivers dangerous undercurrents, her girlfriend's boyfriend jumped in to save her, dragging my mother and her belongings to safety. They were all greatly relieved and pleased to have overcome what they thought was their biggest hurdle towards freedom, however time was of the essence so they did not rejoice for too long before setting out on the next part of their journey. Unfortunately, their heroism was to be short-lived as they did not make it very far before being apprehended and detained by the Austrian border Patrol.

My mother along with her companions were given a choice by the state authorities, they could either return home to their parents in Maribor or they could stay in Austria, on the proviso that they acquired sponsorship through employment. My mother was fortunate enough to have been found immediate employment with an Austrian Countess as her live-in dog-walker and ladies' maid. During her time there the countess grew immensely fond of my mother and decided to help her to fulfil her dream of travelling to a western destination by procuring a false passport for her stating that my mother was eighteen years of age and therefore legally able to travel. She was of course only seventeen years old after having spent a year in the countess's services, but never the less she managed to board a ship headed for Australia along with many other young men and women. When she landed in Australia, she was placed in a migration camp in Victoria called "Bonegilla." She left Bonegilla to live in Melbourne in a share house under the supervision of an older widowed female, she was my mother's custodian of sorts. It was during this time that she was introduced through a mutual acquaintance to my father, they were married not long after.

From Melbourne they moved to South Australia, it was here that my father began a career in the hospitality industry, he worked several jobs simultaneously as a bus-boy and dish-washer at several bars and restaurants. However, it was not long before he became a cook and barman, he then graduated into becoming a maître d' and later a restaurant/bar manager. He was not content to remain an employee for long, he was harbouring personal aspirations to become the owner of his own enterprise. He learned everything he could about the industry he was in and it was not long before he opened his own establishment called the "Golden Eagle" it was a restaurant, cabaret and striptease nightclub. It was one of the first of its' kind to make its debut in Adelaide, which was a town also ironically known as the "city of churches." Having experienced success with the "Golden Eagle" he quite quickly followed up by opening a restaurant simply called "Steven's restaurant". My parents and my two older brothers lived in a renovated loft above the nightclub for a time and it was here that I was conceived and later born, unfortunately it was not long after that my parents were forced to close-down their businesses, going into liquidation. It was due to a combination of pressure from the church lobby groups, the demands of parenthood, protection rackets and poor money management that brought about the end of both those endeavours. From here my parents moved from place to place and city to city, making money and losing money it was a roller coaster ride during which my two younger siblings were born. In my mid teen's, we settled in Melbourne where my father invented and quite successfully manufactured, marketed, and sold several avant-garde products within the glass and glazing industry in which he had been working since the early nineteen seventies.

Our family had finally settled in Melbourne, however we still moved homes and suburbs quite often, until my father built our first family home in a new estate in the suburb of Cheltenham. This became our family home for quite a few years, during which time I was married and had moved to my own home, unfortunately some years later my father had lost this home to the bank when his business went into liquidation. However, he along with his omnipotent disposition and enduring spirit recovered from this collapse managing to not only recoup his losses, but also build a more successful business with the aid of his two eldest sons. He taught us all a valuable lesson through his determination which was to work hard and to "never give in" and "never give up". He showed us that he was indeed a symbol of the proverbial "phoenix rising from the ashes" of his failed ventures, perhaps not necessarily wiser but definitely more determined than ever.

I had attended at least eight different schools as a consequence of the constant moving and can vividly remember being challenged with the continual need to adapt to the differing social environments I was thrust into. Making new friends and settling into new schools was quite often disconcerting and at times anxiety provoking, however leaving the close friendships I had formed behind when we moved on was even more difficult, especially not knowing whether I would be coming back. There are positive and negative aspects that can result from every experience in life and so I believe the inadvertent gain that I had acquired from the constant upheaval was that I developed an internal resiliency and flexibility that held me in good stead with the future challenges and adversities that I had to face. The ability to be resilient and flexible as I came to realise much later on had both served me well and also paradoxically hindered me throughout my life. However, one of the more consequential negative emotional and psychological costs of the constant moving and up-rooting was that I developed an inherent craving for security, stability and a deep desire to belong to and stay rooted in the one place all the more.

When I entered into my mid teens' I started to resent the constant change of environments, I didn't want to leave the friendships that I developed at the schools I attended, I wanted to settle in one place and to feel a sense of belonging. The constant moving had a profound effect on my academic, social and emotional development as I found myself to be a contradictory combination of both shy and introverted at times to being the complete opposite of out-spoken and gregarious at other times. I also without question struggled academically as adjusting to new school environments meant pouring all my energy into surviving the playground and finding my social equals and by that, I mean like-minded peers who were similar in nature. When I turned fifteen it was the first time, I challenged my father on behalf of myself and my other siblings as he was going to move home yet again. I asserted our desire to stay in the high-school that we were currently attending and that we didn't care how many new homes he wanted us to move to, or what suburb we lived in, we refused to move schools again. This intervention worked, so even though we moved house three times in that same area, I was elated to be able to sustain the friendships I had formed. At the age of sixteen I became quite rebellious against the strictures of schooling life and resented authority figures which inevitably found me spending nearly eighty percent of that year "wagging" (playing truant) from school and spending my days with a group of like-minded female and male friends. I found myself getting into trouble at school and sitting in the principal's office more than I did in the class-room which resulted in my having to repeat that scholastic year, which I did so quite successfully.

However, the conventions of traditional schooling continued to frustrate and stifle me, I hated attending school and so I talked my parents into letting me complete year twelve at what was then known as the Caufield Institute of Technology. In this environment I thrived, as all conventional schooling restrictions did not apply, I was free to come and go as I pleased and was able to socialise in between classes without my parent's knowledge. It was during this year that I turned eighteen and it was also during this year that I met my future husband. Our relationship from the very start was somewhat tumultuous as we argued about ridiculous and petty things never realising that this was the beginning of forming the pattern that our relationship was to take in the future. Having both turned eighteen years old that same year we were two youngsters emerging from being teenagers into adulthood. Neither of us possessed any real relationship experience and we had little comparison to draw on other than from our contemporaries and our parents.

Throughout my childhood and into my teen years my parents adhered to a strict moral code where their children were concerned and would mete out physical punishments if they felt it warranted it. It was common practice back in the day to receive a smack on the behind with a hand or wooden spoon and for occasional serious offences one might receive punishment via the belt or the strap across the back of the legs. Even though my mother was a force to be reckoned with, my father was the head of the household as was typical of that era, and so all major decisions were made by him and all major arguments between the siblings in my family were settled with one word from my father. For the most part I do not remember witnessing any significant acts of violence other than what I witnessed on television shows. Bullying at school was the norm and even though I was not completely ignorant about abusers and violence, I knew about as much as my contemporaries knew while growing up. However, I do now know and believe that I was extremely naïve and significantly unacquainted with the dark side of human nature and definitely unprepared to recognise a predator when I met one and so I remained ignorant of its perfidy until I was married.

As was typical of parents brought up through the nineteen fourties and fifties, particularly European parents, they had hopes for my attaining an education, but not much was envisioned for me in terms of a career as I was likely to get married and make my home, children and husband my top priorities. However, until then I led quite a sheltered life from the outside world even though much was expected of me as the oldest daughter in the household. Growing up my most influential role model was my mother, and now looking back I realise that everything I learned through my observations and experiences of her relationship with my father has acted equally as both a positive and negative influence over my life. From her, I had learned to be self-sacrificing (burdened), quite stoic in the face of adversity (to endure), to be unflinchingly loyal to those you love particularly your husband, regardless of their wrong choices and bad behaviour. However, on the plus side, I had learned from observing her to be emotionally, psychologically and physically resilient and through my experience of her I had learned to be affectionate, kind, generous, optimistic and most importantly to have a sense of humour.

I often wondered whether my childhood was setting me up for my later life of preparing me for my later life and I have come to the conclusion that it did both. I believe that it was indeed a dichotomy in the sense that it had simultaneously acted in mutually opposing ways. Upon reflection, with the constant upheaval of having to move homes, schools and states I had experienced instability with my living conditions, I had to suffer the loss of friendships, I had to battle for social acceptance with every new school environment I went into and lastly, I had to struggle to meet the differing interstate academic standards. I was forced by circumstance to learn adaptation and survival skills very early on, as well as developing the social skills necessary to integrate into new and challenging environments. Being quite a shy child from a rather sheltered familial environment meant that I had to learn to acclimatise to the constant changing demands of my new physical and social settings and so by default I had to learn to make new friends. This likely succeeded in strengthening the development of my emotional and psychological elasticity and resilience. The positive influences of my early developmental years, were what prepared me for the challenges of my adult life as I learned to accept, adjust and make the best of whatever circumstances I found myself in. The negative influences of my early developmental years, were that the ever-changing environments and constant upheaval also caused me to develop emotional and psychological insecurities, feelings of inadequacy and a profound need for stability and security, more than likely setting me up to draw in the wrong intimate relationships.

We are the Sum of Many Parts

Responsibilities such as looking after my younger siblings, cleaning and cooking were part of my life since the age of nine, this was common practice for daughters growing up in European households, as you were expected to learn these skills in preparation for your married life as wife and later as a mother. As the oldest daughter, I was expected to be able to make the right choices and decisions for myself and my younger siblings beyond my maturity and experience level, which was very typical of the larger family dynamic from that era. When I got it wrong, I was in trouble, so I learned very early on to take my responsibilities seriously and to put others needs before my own. I later came to understand that it was through my experiences during my early formative developmental years that I formed the belief that to feel good about myself and to raise my self-esteem was through, helping others, being a support for others and being forgiving, understanding and loyal to others. These "qualities" (character traits) became an intrinsic part of my psychological make-up and so I viewed these parts of myself as being virtuous, something to be proud of and a forum from which I could receive praise and acceptance. This provided the nourishment that fed my self-esteem and at the same time supported elevating the ego-ideal I held of myself, sustaining my need to feel accepted, special, loved and respected.

Yes, upon face value these are great qualities to have, however they are only great qualities to have if they are tempered with a healthy balance of receiving these qualities equally from others for yourself. When you are the one doing all the giving without receiving then in the long term you will undoubtably find yourself exhausted, lonely, unappreciated, disappointed, disillusioned and resentful. I was playing the role of "good mother" for everyone else not understanding that I needed to be "good mother" for myself as well. I had not learned to directly receive the unconditional affection, approval and love I needed unless it was through acts of selflessness for others. However contrarily, these needs felt somewhat fulfilled although in an oddly vicarious manner.

Through meeting others needs and demands I was able to feel good about myself which I mistakenly interpreted as receiving love from those I was in service too.

This early developmental "ideal" that I adopted fostered the birth of a character structure known as the "masochistic" or "burdened enduring" character structure, which took root and over time made its home in my psyche, becoming a formidable and predominant part of my psychological make-up (refer to character structure book one). This defence mechanism although not the only one I possessed was a governing negative influence over my life as the need to be emotionally connected to or loved by another human-being equated to the loss of my personal choices. I became self-sacrificing in my service to others, forever putting those I worked with, my family and some of my more demanding friends needs and wants before my own. The need to experience approval from the significant others in my life was the lynch pin that held my fragile ego-identity together, without it I would experience feelings of deep shame, guilt, self-doubt, insecurity and failure. The fact that I couldn't be "good mother" for myself created a deep void that became, what is referred to in psychotherapy as a "shadow" or "disowned" part of myself. This part of me that I didn't possess needed fulfilment and was actively seeking it outside myself from other sources. It was an unconsciously driven need looking for a home, which it found in all my relationships with others including my friends, family, work associates and of course in my intimate partner.

Being "good mother" or "good father" to oneself is necessary in a healthy psyche it refers to the ability to be able to parent oneself from within in a healthy and adaptive manner. This helps us to balance what we give to and receive from others in all areas of our lives, physically, psychologically and emotionally. Our inner parent/s are usually modelled on our upbringing, which is based on how and by whom we were parented combined with the sociological (cultural, environmental and religious), economic and physiological conditions throughout our childhood and adolescence. The absence of a positive inner parent or the development of a negative inner parent becomes part of our psychological framework and influences every decision we make and every action we take and determines the quality of the life we live. In my case, I lacked a strong positive inner role model that would have supported me making healthy and balanced decisions concerning caring for myself and allowing for my own needs and aspirations to be fulfilled.

It is a natural and innate yearning in all human-being to be accepted, approved of and loved by others and most importantly by oneself. However, if you do not know how to provide these needs directly to yourself then you will likely strive to seek that approval, acceptance and love vicariously through being in service to others. Without the positive influence of "good mother" in my psyche there was a much-needed part of me that was missing, my inability to nurture myself created an unconscious, negative "needy" and vulnerable self as a result. This aspect of myself is disowned in a sense (not consciously aware of or acknowledged), becoming an elusive shadow aspect of myself that I craved personally but projected outwardly onto significant others in my life. In other words, because I could not directly care for, love myself or gratify my own needs and desires I was either unconsciously drawn to those that could or contrarily disliked those that could. I found people who were needy in an overtly highly emotionally expressive and dependent manner, hard to cope with, they annoyed and irritated me, I could not understand or tolerate their neediness. This was my personal dichotomy; on the one hand I married a needy and self-gratifying person and on the other I openly vehemently disliked others who showed signs of possessing these same qualities.

In order to avoid or counteract personally experiencing any of these unwanted emotions, I developed various psychological defences (refer to victim defences book 1). These defences took root during my childhood and evolved over time as I grew and combined with my life experiences, had matured solidifying themselves into hardened unshakable safeguards. One of the most significant defences that manifested in my attempt to circumvent feeling my true needs and any vulnerability associated with those needs was that I developed an "all-dealing and no-feeling" approach to the challenges in my life. Being emotionally detached was a means of survival for me, it helped me to set boundaries and protected me from experiencing powerlessness. By numbing my feelings, I could get the job done and escape experiencing my own and other people's emotional discomfort or pain as well as avoid feelings of dejection, anxiety, failure and fear.

Two other powerful avoidant defences that ruled my life were firstly, that I had become extremely highly organised, bordering on occasion of being obsessive and compulsive in nature. I took immense pride in getting the "supposed" impossible done. This was driven by a deep need to be in control in order to counteract and/or avoid feelings of chaos, powerlessness and inadequacy. It supported my need to live an ordered life and provided me with the illusion that I was in charge of my life and not at the mercy of its' dictates. Secondly, I set extremely high moral and behavioural standards for myself, continuously striving for but never attaining perfection in all my endeavours whether it was related to my personal, home, workplace, or social relationships. I expected much from myself and those who surrounded me, however ironically, I never expected or received it from my husband, I rationalised and minimised his actions.

He was given much leeway, and it was from him I was longingly seeking approval, acceptance and love even though he was both incapable of giving it to me or predisposed to do so. In fact, his reciprocation was minimal and even though on the surface he appeared to others to be confident, ambitious, gregarious and self-possessed, he was fundamentally deeply needy, immature and insecure underneath. His character type fit in perfect with my own as I was drawn both unconsciously to his young and needy self (an aspect of my shadow) and consciously to his outward projection of the self-assured, bold and outgoing self. I accepted small morsels of affection and praise from him throughout our relationship and I accepted these scraps like a person who was dying of hunger and these scraps were keeping me alive. The smallest bit of praise or show of affection would wash warmly over me, it was all I needed to go on, and even though this reflects badly on his character it also exposes my own incapacity to ask for, or receive more and reveals my deeply held unacknowledged feelings of unworthiness. This highlights the fact that it takes either opposing or similar dysfunctions of both the individuals involved, to be working in unison to keep a maladaptive relationship together. He was incapable of providing the care, love and affection that I needed and craved due to his psychopathic/narcissistic character traits and I was unaware that I needed and deserved more due to my masochistic/burdened enduring character traits.

I have referred to the term "shadow" on a few occasions and would like to further explain as simply as possible what I mean when I use this term. Technically our shadow is known as an unconscious aspect of our personality that our conscious ego does not identify in itself. According to Jungian based psychology, shadow aspects of oneself can be positive or negative in nature however they are largely perceived to be negative and considered to be the least desirable characteristics of ones' personality. Everyone carries a "shadow" and the less it is embodied (knowingly accepted or acknowledged) in an individual's conscious life, the deeper in the unconscious it presides. A shadow aspect of ourselves is an unwanted aspect of our personality, we can remain in ignorance of its presence (known as the "shadow archetype") or we can reject it. Either way it is likely to be perceived as a personal inferiority in oneself which is psychologically projected outwardly onto another recognising it be a moral deficiency in someone else.

The Attraction

I met my future husband in the autumn of 1980 at the iconic Melbourne nightclub known as "Chasers discotheque" on a night out with some girlfriends, I was eighteen at the time, we met briefly as it was quite late. He was the epitome of the phrase "tall dark and handsome" and I found his boldness and his European dark looks attractive and so for the first time I gave a stranger my work address. I did not own a mobile phone and I was definitely not going to give him my home phone number as I had a strict father who would have "flipped out" if he called. I worked part-time (Friday nights and Saturday mornings) as a waitress in a friend of the family's café in the city. So, I gave him my work address to which he promised to pop in and see me the following week. There was an instant attraction between us and so we started dating and after about three months our relationship became sexual in nature, a natural progression or inevitability if you like for two young, healthy burgeoning adults.

As we personally grew in connectedness, we also became more and more enmeshed in each other's lives, I met his friends all of whom were from a European background and I clicked with them in a profound way. However, he found it difficult to embrace my friends most of whom were from Anglo-Saxon backgrounds as he found them to be too culturally different from himself and he could not accept the differences between himself and them. As time went on it became more and more difficult for me to sustain my original personal friendships as he consistently complained and protested whenever I planned to see them with or without him. He had something negative to say about each one of them and it soon became a constant bone of contention that was wearing on our relationship and personally distressing for me. I slowly but surely started to separate from my friendship group and became more entrenched with the friends he approved of without consciously realising that I was moving into his world. Meeting his family had been seamless, I fit in immediately and it wasn't long before I developed a strong relationship with his parents and his siblings, which corresponded with my own European background and was supported by my easy-going and accepting nature.

However, it was not so seamless when I introduced him to my family, as my father was not ready to accept that his daughter was ready for interacting with the male species in that way and secondly, he was not ready to accept a new male member into the fold. My mother and siblings on the other hand were quite happy for me to start dating and so he was invited to dinner despite my father's reluctance to meet him. It was a difficult first meet to say the least and it set the precedence for his future relationship with my father as I can remember the underlying tension and clash of unspoken wills throughout the night. The result of two narcissistic personalities coming together in silent opposition both vying for control, one was my father who was not ready to relinquish control of his daughter and the other was my potential life-partner who was competing for the right to take control of his daughter.

Many years later during my training as a therapist, I was tasked with researching my family tree for an assignment, its' purpose was to understand and make connections from our past to our present-day life. During this process I can distinctly remember referring to an image that depicted that first meeting between my father and my ex-husband who was my boyfriend at that time. The visual that instantly came to mind was of two wolves circling each other, teeth bared, both taking each other's measure, ready to fight for what they wanted. However, despite their initial meet and mutual dislike, we continued to date for about two years and then became engaged during which time my siblings and my mother grew to like if not love him and my father and my fiancé grudgingly came to accept each other to a degree and for a period of time.

I was barely eighteen years old when I first met my partner and had literally turned twenty-one years old on the night we were married, I was just emerging from a rather cocooned and conservative background and hadn't yet developed an identity or a solid sense of self. In fact, I was innocently idealistic, trusting of those I loved and cared for and extremely naïve, so I definitely was not prepared for dealing with a volatile relationship or understanding this complex and temperamental man. However, I loved him with all the innocence and passion of youth and I believed he loved me with the same intensity. I was excited about our future and thought my girlhood dreams were coming to fruition, I imagined running my own home, having children and creating a family, while having a loving, caring husband and father for my children by my side who shared the

31

same ideals as my own. I was also secretly thrilled to get out from under the constant supervision of my parents and in particular my fathers antiquated rules and regulations.

My partner had come into the relationship with sexual experience having lost his virginity at a young age, however I had gifted him with mine. I wasn't thinking wedding bells when we started our intimate relationship as I was a young, curious and healthy teenager and this was a natural progression of our developing connection, but I was thinking and feeling that we had a future together. As time went on, I thought myself to be in love with him and promptly projected all my dreams of "happy ever after" onto this relationship. I later came to know that he was not in the least bit idealistic about our relationship, for him it was a means of having his sexual needs met on a regular basis and it was a bonus that I fit in and was liked by his family and friends. He liked me very much and he was definitely attracted to me but he wasn't thinking long-term until our relationship was tested with a sexual indiscretion committed by him. I am not sure to this day why he felt compelled to tell me about it, however once I was told I promptly broke up with him, he responded by relentlessly pursuing me. This pursual culminated in a magnanimous demonstration by him, it was an offer of marriage, he wanted our future to be together, proposing that we get engaged, I was surprised but thrilled and of course said yes. The confession about his indiscretion was the first and last time that he told me the truth about anything, our life to follow was full of half-truths and outright lies.

The question is why pursue me when he had a perfect way out of the relationship and would be free to play the field as he was inclined to want to do. The answer is of course that his ego over-estimated my attachment to him not expecting me to break off our relationship as a result of his indiscretion. This triggered his narcissistic instincts and I believe he decided that we were not going to end that way, he was not ready to let me go. I was malleable, I was innocent and naïve and this was part of the criteria that fit in with his manipulative, controlling and dominating personality. He could lie to me and get away with it and probably had consistently lied to me from the onset of our relationship. He was typical of a "sexual narcissist", someone who was driven to seek sexual gratification without emotional attachment and therefore not inclined to engage in a long-term or committed relationships. However, he was a sexual narcissist who also came from a conservative ethnic culture with catholic religious overtones, who would have felt compelled to get married at some time in his future, needing his family's approval and wanting at some point to father his own children. This had helped to support his decision to make the grand gesture of committing to an engagement with me, and it did help that I fit in perfectly with his family and friends, they liked me and I had already forged strong bonds with many of them.

We were engaged for about a year before we married, however during this brief period our relationship was rather mercurial, a rollercoaster ride of highs and lows interspersed with senseless arguments. It was a mixture of amazing fun and joyous occasions with friends and family to ridiculously petty arguments and deeply disturbing quarrels. His repeated attempts at manipulation and consistent attempts at establishing supremacy over me caused us to take breaks in our relationship and at one point we had called it quits, this lasted about two weeks. Despite our disagreements and differences, we seemed to be irrevocably drawn to each other and later inevitably destined for a world of heartache and pain. We shared a physical attraction to each other, and as time went on became further intimately attached, I thought our shared European backgrounds were significantly similar, and was under the impression that we shared the same morals, ideals and work ethic. However, unbeknownst to me he actually was not as accepting of our cultural and differing family dynamics as I was led to believe, comparing it to his own and finding it flawed. This was compounded by the fact that he had harboured a hidden, deep animosity towards my father from the onset of our relationship that never changed but rather festered until it later became hatred. He felt the compelling need to change me as our relationship evolved so that I fit into his version of the perfect girlfriend, wife, hostess, mother and daughter in-law. In order to achieve this end, he entered into an unrelenting campaign to make those changes happen.

Being in a relationship with an abuser who among his other negative patterns of behaviour, was also afflicted with the "Peter Pan" and "Madonna-Whore" syndromes (refer to book one) left me psychologically overwhelmed, emotionally drained, and physically exhausted. The lack of reciprocal respect, care, consideration and affection left me feeling extremely neglected and at the same time it exposed a deeper, hidden and uncomfortable part of myself that paradoxically felt unworthy of receiving those things. I never had time to reflect on what was missing in my life and I did not know that I deserved better, I was "starved" for the acceptance, warmth, intimacy and real connection which I would never receive from him. His powerful persona was all-consuming and overshadowed all our conflicts it was as if he had siphoned the life-force out of me, always leaving me feeling confused, dazed, and drained of energy. His narcissistic personality disorder required that he be my number one priority above all others including myself, our extended family and later even our children. He needed me to be his "mother figure" when it came time to forgive him for his indiscretions out-side our marriage and for his abusive behaviour towards me inside our marriage.

My fear of rejection and my longing for acceptance and validation fuelled my "Wendy Syndrome", this combined with my partners inability to grow up "Peter Pan Syndrome" was one of the underlying but significant issues that drew us together. These disorders kept us together with neither of us aware that we both possessed a set of emotional and psychological complexes that were a significant driving force behind our relationship. During our relationship throughout all the drama, I played my "Wendy" role (good mother), I was understanding, self-sacrificing, loyal and most of all particularly forgiving, without receiving the same considerations from my "Peter Pan" (eternal child) partner. He expected the archetypal "good mother" the "Madonna", which he received and when he was "naughty", he acted like a sheepish child, expecting a wrap over the knuckles and to forget his transgressions regardless of their seriousness (refer to book one, Peter Pan, Wendy, and Madonna/whore Syndrome's).

Unfortunately for me, because I was innocent and had little relationship experience my insecurities and fears were transparent, providing my husband (abuser) the material with which to exploit and devalue me. Even though we were the same age he was already an experienced predator having honed his skills of manipulation from a young age, he was driven by his primal instinct which was to satiate his needs first and foremost and to dominate and control his environment and those around him. He had little intimate relationship experience of the non-sexual kind himself as we were both eighteen when we met, however we were contrarily worlds apart in the way in which we were reared. He was taught to be mistrustful and suspicious of others motives and that to be taken advantage of by someone (made a fool of) was the worst thing a man could let happen to himself. In his culture this was considered to be a serious failure that reflected badly on a man's character, a sign of his naivety and stupidity. This belief perpetuated an already burgeoning cynical outlook towards life that likely started in his childhood causing him to act in a defensive manner so as not to disappoint his father and thereby experience any shame that may result from such mistake. He decided he was better off being the one taking advantage of others so as to avoid being taken advantage of himself.

I can remember feeling like I couldn't tell my parents, siblings or those friends I was closest to about what I was experiencing because I felt a deep sense of irrational personal shame and failure which I didn't understand but was both unconsciously and consciously driven by. In my inexperience I really believed that at some time in the future he would change his behaviour of his own accord and that he would eventually also mellow in nature. I rationalised that our relationship would right itself and the abuse would stop if specific external events would take place to make us happy. These events were always in the future and started with statements such as "if only" we had more money or "when we" buy our first home or "when he" establishes his business or "when we" have children etc. etc. I was firm in the belief that there would be a "happy ever after" for us, this idealistic belief served to keep me looking to the future and played a big part in downplaying current abusive events.

I was raised in an era and environment that was influenced by strong misogynistic and chauvinistic elements, a patriarchal society of which my father was a product. My mother like many other women of her generation was forced to accept her husband's edicts, and more often than not had responded with compliance, stoicism and perhaps a little secret resentment. The message to my developing psyche was quite clear though, I had learned through observation and by absorption on an unconscious level to accept and endure my burdens in silence. This unconscious injunction to be "silent" ruled me throughout my life keeping my authentic voice trapped behind an ego façade that constantly sought approval and acceptance from others. This hindered the development of a true self, forcing the creation of a persona that was constructed from the sum of my parental and archetypal societal influences and expectations. Like my mother and I imagine my female ancestors before her, I was either actively discouraged or not permitted to indulge my genuine feelings or thoughts on any matter of significance but rather navigated by an unseen but powerful patriarchal force. The male dominated society in which I grew up would subtly and/or directly purposefully allude to female limitations and never female aptitudes and my husband along with many of his cronies were brought up to believe that women were less than their male counterparts.

The Abuse

The physical and verbal abuse started from very early on in the marriage almost straight after our two-week honeymoon. We had many arguments before we were married during our engagement, however there was never any evidence of threatening behaviour or physical violence, our arguments were psychological and emotional in nature, I thought our arguments the norm. I never considered any of his behaviour in terms of it being abusive as I had a limited concept of what constituted abusive behaviour at that time, other than it would have to be physical in nature and it would leave some kind of evidence of the violence. I cannot remember ever witnessing my father being physically abusive to my mother, however they did have verbal altercations that would always end with them both sulking and the possible slamming of bedroom and cupboard doors and/or my mother engaging in treating my father with the silent treatment. The silent treatment could go on for days until they made up, I cannot remember what the arguments were over, however knowing my father's penchant for foolhardy risk-taking monetary ventures, I can imagine what the content of those arguments would have been.

In the first years of our marriage, we fought consistently over everything, he wanted his home run exactly like his mother ran hers and his life to be exactly as it was when he lived with his parents. He wanted me to be a clone of his mother, his ideal of the perfect wife (housekeeper, carer, cook) and according to him I was falling short, this caused much upheaval as we struggled to adjust to a life together. Within the first twelve months I was quickly learning about his volatile temper, he wasn't happy with the way I performed household duties this included my cooking, the way I cleaned, the way I folded his clothes and in particular the way I ironed. According to him I was seriously lacking in the domestic arena and he consistently compared me to his mother, he especially could not accept if his shirts were not ironed to an expert standard. His clothing had to be immaculate as his appearance meant everything to him and so it was critical to get this right or he would become infuriated. His angry tirades escalated over time transforming into further violence with him throwing things either around the house or at me. In one incident he ripped the wardrobe door right off its hinges and threw it across the room, on another occasion because I didn't move fast enough, I was hit in the ankle with frozen food that caused me to faint and resulted in an injury that I nursed for a few weeks. Our arguments also centred around many other issues, money becoming a primary and persistent matter of contention that would dog our relationship throughout its existence from the beginning to the end. If it wasn't about the lack of it, it would be about how, when, where and on whom it would be spent, money was his god and he aspired to have great wealth and property. Don't get me wrong I wanted a home, nice things and the trappings of a comfortable life too and was just as prepared as he was to work for it and I did.

The abuse in our relationship seemed to become cyclic in nature increasing in frequency, nastiness, and unpredictability as the years went on. Anything could set him off, there were some things I had learned were his pet hates but most of the time his temper would burst out of him and I never saw it coming. It could have ignited from an incident related to his work, social life, family or within our personal relationship and could be as minor as a slight or something major that upset him it didn't matter, he would go from zero to sixty in a minute. His tirades would continue until he became physically tired, he was like a child having a tantrum. These outbursts started to increase in intensity and before long evolved into physical violence and verbal cruelty and seemed to always be directed at me. I was always the target for his anger and rage regardless of the cause or origin of his upset and just because he needed someone to blame. He used me to vent his frustrations, failures and disappointments onto, it was his only way of dealing with them as he had no other life skills to call on.

He felt the need to continually verbally belittle me and malign members of my family in order to raise his own self-esteem and to boost his feelings of superiority. He especially seemed to take great delight in maligning my lineage as if being "Yugoslavian" was in itself a fault and certainly one I could not change. It did not stop there he would denigrate both of my parents and my brothers, constantly espousing that they were deficient in some way. He deemed certain members of my family an embarrassment because of their outward displays of flamboyance, whilst at the same time praising his own family, elevating himself and his family's "supposed humility" to lofty heights. This heightened my feelings of inadequacy because yes, the truth is there were many times that my father embarrassed my mother, my siblings and me with his bragging, his fabrications, and his exaggerations. Even though I loved my parents, I desperately desired and needed my husband's approval and acceptance, and so over time came to see his parents as the "ideal" parents, in particular his mother. Without realising it I set about adopting some of her behaviours, I learned to cook his favourite dishes, in fact she taught me how to make authentic southern Italian cuisine from scratch and with the same degree of proficiency. Her self-sacrificing disorder encouraged my already existing self-denying disorder and keeping the peace in the family and ensuring that the male members of our household were well fed and content in every way was paramount.

Unknowingly I had polarised his parents and their family dynamic at the ideal end of the behavioural spectrum and my parents and family dynamic at the other. This did not in any way diminish the affection and love I held for my parents and siblings but it did make me want to change myself. However, having said that both of our parents possessed many similar characteristics, they had both worked hard all their lives and they were both generous, kind, and caring. His dislike for my parents made itself apparent very early on in our marriage even though they never interfered in our relationship whatsoever, unfortunately as time went on what seemed like mild dislike grew to become loathing and contempt. He disapproved of their values which he believed were purportedly different from his own and he absolutely despised my father. I can understand him not wanting to listen to my dad's exaggerated bullshit, the rest of the family myself included, did not want to hear his nonsense either. However, as is typical of an abuser's "modus operandi" he took the opportunity to use this as a way of driving a wedge between ourselves and my family, by consistently vilifying them. He was inflexible and unaccepting of those who were different from himself, he might tolerate them but he would not accept them.

My need to feel better about myself and to support the ego-ideal that I was developing of being the "perfect wife, hostess and house keeper" centred on getting approval from my husband, family, and our friends. This led to my attempting to emulate his mother and distancing myself from my own, although at that time I was not consciously aware that I was doing this. However, as is the case with a psychopathic/narcissistic abuser, nothing I did was ever "good enough", no matter how hard I tried to please him he would find fault with everything I did or said. I can remember we had a huge argument in our first year of marriage because I didn't fold his socks in the same way his mother used to, and on one occasion he ripped to pieces four of five of his shirts in a fit of rage because the one he wanted was in the ironing basket. All his actions were really about his own feelings of inadequacy fostered by his deeply held unconscious belief that he was essentially unworthy. To counteract these negative feelings and to build his self-esteem he would put down or denigrate others, highlighting others faults made him feel better about himself. The tearing of his shirts was more due to his feelings of low self-esteem about his fluctuating weight gain, something that was a constant personal source of frustration and dissatisfaction for him. This behaviour showcased his inability to process these unwelcome emotions in a mature and adaptive manner and therefore he responded in the only way he knew how which was an outward expression of rage.

He was always at the mercy of his own volatile and unresolved emotions, unable to understand what drove him into these rages or why, and he had no desire to question or change himself. In his mind everything that went wrong in his life, all his disappointments and unfulfilled dreams were centred outside himself, he was incapable of self-reflection. We both never understood it at the time but I believe he played a victim of sorts, as if circumstances beyond his control and other people were responsible for his missed opportunities and set-backs. He never ever took responsibility for himself or his abusive actions towards me but he did show contrition on occasion after cooling off and only when he believed it was a necessary reparation if he thought he had gone too far or he had left a longer lasting injury.

His relentless manipulative attempts at isolating me from external influences were successful, I eventually estranged myself from my family and he had attained the position he was vying for, which was to become the most important person in my life. He acquired the dominant and controlling position he needed and wanted and the most substantial bonus for him was that there was no significant other person in our lives that could interfere with our relationship or gainsay his actions. You are probably curious as to how does someone go about separating and/or isolating a person from those closest to them to that degree. The answer is not simple but more complex than you might imagine, it again involves two maladaptive psychological complexes working together to co-create dysfunction, which will vary in degree of intensity and type of dysfunction, making it unique to each relationship. In my relationship it was layered with several underlying issues, it involved my feelings of low self-esteem which were being fostered by my unconscious belief that I was unworthy and undeserving. He used my low self-esteem against me, compounding my negative feelings about myself with consistent comments that were designed to belittle and depreciate me which were paradoxically driven by his own feelings of unworthiness and failure. Some of his disparaging comments were direct hits in which he pulled no punches, and some were more subtle in the form of innuendo and sarcasm, all however were aimed at highlighting that I was "less than him" and he was "more than me".

His displays of violence included shoving me against walls, holding me there with one hand wrapped around my throat while leaning his body and his face into me as close as he can get while he ranted, raved and threatened me. Holding me by the throat was his way of letting me know that he could take my life at any time and that he was in charge. When he'd finally let me go, it would be followed by hours of being verbally criticised, belittled and yelled at. His tirade may have originated with a particular issue that had irritated or "pissed him off", but would always end up being about me personally, my lineage and/or my family. There was no possibility of circumventing the trajectory of his rage once ignited, I knew there was no escaping his wrath and there was absolutely nothing I could do or say to placate him. He had to vent his anger and frustration regardless of its' origin and nothing was going to stop him and what might start off as an angry rant could build into a full-blown fury within him without provocation. This was a common outcome, as the more he dwelled on whatever subject had him enthralled the angrier he became. I learned very early on to remain silent or to say as little as possible to him when he was raging at me, even though he asked me rhetorical questions and made untrue and exaggerated accusations about me and my family. Responding to him in any way only served to fuel his anger, even when I was forced to agree with him it incited more anger, nothing I said or didn't say could stop the course of an abusive episode. I learned to remain as passive as possible and not show any emotion, this also angered him, however the episodes were much shorter if I remained expressionless, repressing all emotion.

I rarely showed my anxiety, fear, anger, disbelief or my physical and emotional pain no matter what he said or did to me, there were occasions however where this wasn't possible of course. Most of the violence that he perpetrated was used as a means of keeping me trapped while he held a menacing

40

stance over me, providing him with a dominant and controlling position in which he could rant and rave to his heart's content and he did. Over the years I have been slapped, knocked around, I was thrown against walls and into furniture, I was hit with objects that he threw at me, I was punched a couple of times and on one occasion I was hit repeatedly with his belt. He had a habit of grabbing me by my upper arms to either bodily shake me or to move me to where he wanted me to be. Over the years I never sustained a broken limb but likely had a few fractures, I had a black eye on one occasion that I can remember and plenty of bruises, however they were in places that for the most part, were easily hidden by clothing. On several occasions, I didn't even know I had a bruise until someone else noticed it, to which I would respond with a casual shrug as if I didn't know how it got there. Going to bed with him after or during a tirade was not only alarming, it was exhausting, he would more often than not rant and rave for hours. My eyes would stay fixated on the ceiling over our bed, quite often I found myself counting the little rosettes that adorned the ceiling rose, which I repeated over and over again, while silently hoping and praying that he would tire out and let me sleep. This was my way of coping with the abuse he was hurling at me, it was a small way in which I was trying to protect myself.

These night-time tirades were the worst because I had to get up at 6.15am during the week to get ready for work, he never cared what time it was when he wanted my attention, there was no stopping him from having his say. He would not let me leave the bedroom and so I had no choice but to listen to him. Sometimes he just verbally berated me until he fell asleep and other times, he would physically push me out of the bed and onto the floor but would not let me leave as he needed to continue yelling at me. I would have to wait until he fell asleep and then slip into the bed so that I could get a few hours of sleep. There were times when we were either heading out or heading home from somewhere and out of anger/rage he would stop the car we were driving in and tell me to get out or push me out and then he would drive off leaving me stranded. He would then come back looking for me forcing me back into the car only to continue to abusing me. At home, he would end some arguments by telling me to pack my bags and get out, he would push me about demanding I pack my clothes, but of course he had no intention of actually letting me leave the premises.

However, there were two occasions that occurred where I had made attempts to leave him, in the first incident I had left in my car late at night after an argument, he responded by jumping into his car and following me, driving erratically then cutting me off and forcing me to return home. On this occasion he dragged me into the house then punched and belted me, raging on till the early hours of dawn. The next incident occurred a few weeks later, we had just found out that my father who I was working for at the time had put a property that he owned (a home) into my name without my knowledge or consent. My father then later proceeded to take a large loan to prop his failing business using this same property as collateral and again this was without my knowledge or consent. When his business went into liquidation the bank came knocking at my door looking to seize and sell this property, they wanted a quick sale and had a buyer ready to pay the exact amount of the loan repayment which would completely cover moneys owed. However, when I apprised my father of the banks intentions and that I did not have a choice in the matter, he was enraged telling me not to sign anything and that the bank had no right to take this property. He was wrong of course, the bank had every right to sell this property but because I had spent the better half of a week trying to make him understand, we had lost the buyer. Long story short the property was sold a few weeks later but at a loss and I was left with having to pay the deficit. My father was deeply incensed with me for having sold the property and was not prepared to pay the shortfall to the bank, leaving me to foot the bill.

My father had betrayed my trust abusing his standing in my life for his own gains, however this was the least of my problems. I had no time to process what he had done to me personally as my husband flew into one of the biggest rages that I had ever experienced with him when he found out that my father had put us into debt. My husband was a disciple who worshipped at the altar of the god "money" he never under any circumstances coped well when he lost it. The debt totalled twenty-five thousand dollars, to which two of my siblings had stepped in to help, reducing it to fifteen thousand dollars, my husband was infuriated. I can absolutely understand him feeling angry, disappointed and upset with my father and can even understand him not wanting to have anything to do with my father. However, does this justify the actions that were to follow when he let his rage have free run. I could not help but think that this situation although unexpected was what my husband had been waiting for, a big enough reason to create an unbreachable divide between ourselves and my family. On this significant occasion, there was no room for any rational discussion, he let his fury take full possession of his faculties. His wrath was not to be denied, he responded that night by loading his hunting rifle with ammunition, grabbing me by winding his fist into my hair. He then dragged me down our long hallway to the front door, where he proceeded to tell me that he was going to shoot my whole family in front of me while I watched.

This traumatic incident had embedded itself in my memory and I guess it will be there forever, however fortunately due to the passage of time and therapeutic treatment it now does not carry with it any harmful or distressing emotion. I can now recall this traumatic event without the weight of the life-changing tormenting and frightening emotional and psychological affect it had inflicted on me in the many years that followed its initiation. It was during this incident that I recognised almost immediately the seriousness of the situation, a sudden life altering realisation dawned on me with absolute clarity, I must not see or contact my family again. He had that crazed look in his eyes that always haunted me, it was the look of a person on the edge of sanity, absorbed by his inner demons and consumed by his rage (I had not spoken to, or seen my family for the next twenty years), I was twenty-seven years old at the time. During this incident I had "dissociated" out of shock (although I wasn't aware at the time), an overwhelming feeling of being disembodied came over me and I can remember a part of me looking down at both of us from above, watching what was happening. I was stunned into immobility, my body locking into "freeze" mode momentarily suspending me in time and space, muting the fear and making me feel as if the whole experience was surreal. At first, I could not hear what he was saying to me, it was as if my mind had muffled all sound perhaps unconsciously preparing me for my next move, I was staring at his face watching his lips move but there was no sound. Slowly as if coming out of a trance that part of me which was observing the scene below started to engage, bringing back to life my hearing and my ability to think. Even though I remained in a somewhat dreamlike state not feeling the terror that I knew was lurking just beneath the surface, my mind had become acutely aware of the gravity of the situation triggering my innate autonomic compulsion for self-preservation to kick in.

I frantically began assessing the precariousness of the situation and weighing up the probability of his intentions, while closely observing his every micro-movement in order to prepare some kind of response. A kaleidoscope of previous abusive scenes and their outcomes flowed through my mind in an effort to assist me in my desperate search for an appropriate response that could effectively placate him and simultaneously diffuse the situation. However, his threats of lethal violence against my family were on a whole new level than I had ever experienced with him before and not something I readily knew how to deal with. My previous responses to his violence were limited to a show of passivity and a blank wall of silence which I instinctively knew would not work for me right now. I had to respond in a way that was distinctly dramatic to break through the red haze of rage that was driving his actions and that he would accept as real contrition.

I responded by literally forcing out tears, feigning remorse and babbling out incoherent platitudes telling him what I thought he needed to hear. This worked, it stopped him from going any further, he put down his rifle but paid out on me for the rest of the night. From that night onwards I can remember obsessively thinking about that rifle and how to get it removed from our home, I was always worried that in a fit of rage he would turn it on me. Suffice to say he never again loaded a shotgun and threatened me or my family with it, simply because he didn't need to, the message was loud and clear, I cannot leave him without sustaining dire, possibly life-threatening consequences, I had to stay and make the best of the situation for now. I was profoundly and indelibly affected by this event, it altered me on a cellular level destabilising my personal sense of security and safety and contributed to creating an overall weariness and distrust of all men.

I was not remotely equipped to process the effects of the ordeal, nor was I able to manage the bone-jarring fear that it instilled in my psyche. This fear was a poison that ran deep, its pervasive little tentacles had crawled into every area of my life influencing every decision I made and every action I took from that day forward. I became hyper-vigilant both unconsciously and consciously always on the look-out for potentially dangerous situations, not trusting anyone. Looking back, I believe he had no intention of killing my family, there was no way he would have gone to gaol where the real tough guys were housed, but I was not to learn this about him until considerably later in my life. His rage at me on these two significant occasions was a combination of being infuriated at me for even considering leaving him and it was also fuelled by the animosity he harboured for my father. He was never going to let me leave him and return to my family fold, he likely viewed this as a substantial loss on his part in his narcissistic game of ownership between himself and his number one adversary "my father". He regarded me as his property, something he owned among all his other possessions perhaps believing that he had invested his time, money and energy into our relationship and he was not prepared to part with his property, nor was he going to allow a split of the marital assets. I had resigned myself to the fact that the only way to survive was to make the best of the situation, while silently clinging to the hope that at some point in the future he would mellow and that I would reunite with my family.

Our marriage lasted twenty-four years, during which time the two greatest joys of my life came into being, my daughter and my son. They became my inspiration to create the best life possible for them and triggered a desire in me to want a better life for myself. I felt like I was born to be a mother, it was instinctual for me and I had a lot of love to give and thoroughly enjoyed everything to do with homemaking and I especially loved to cook for my family and our friends. I became the consummate hostess at our many dinner parties, taking responsibility for everything to do with our home and our social life, my husband never helped with rearing the children or the household duties. I cleaned, cooked, looked after the garden, did the washing, all the shopping, paid the bills, did the school runs and after school runs, took my children everywhere they needed to go including their social life. I did the gift buying for every occasion and for everyone and I organised all social functions and birthday parties. I also worked part time and was my husband's personal errands girl, his masseuse, his nurse, his lover and his mother. I was highly organised and ran a tight ship, I prided myself on my ability to do it all, however the more responsibility I took on the more he expected from me. I did my best to create a life that I thought I could be happy in, deluding myself into believing that at some point there would be a pay-off and that my sacrifices would have been worth it. On one significant level, I felt fulfilled, this was in my role as mother, I found it fundamentally rewarding to love and be loved by my children and I treasured everything to do with motherhood even the challenges.

However, at the same time my relationship with my husband was a constant source of anxiety, stress and emotional pain. Even though I felt rewarded within my role as mother, I was equally unhappy and disenchanted in a profound way within my relationship with my husband. He was rarely there for my children in the way in which a father needed to be, his absences were felt deeply by my children despite my efforts to compensate for the loss. During our marriage my husband built up his business to a reasonably successful level while we journeyed with the highs and lows that creating a business requires, and so with this also came his professional failures and triumphs. He was abusive when he wasn't coping and I was the recipient of that abuse it would come in waves but we could hardly go a month without a significant abusive occurrence.

We had a reasonably busy social life as a couple, as a family (with our children) and as individuals. However, he was an avid football fan and so he would religiously go to football games with mates and then drinks afterwards, he played golf most weekends which involved drinks with the boys afterwards, he was a hunter and so this involved weekends away with the boys and then of course there was his work and gym commitments. I was both extremely relieved when he wasn't around feeling lighter and calmer as I was free from his constant physical, psychological and emotional demands and at the same time, I was paradoxically plagued with loneliness and deep feelings of unfulfillment and disillusionment.

What I didn't know at the time was that of course I was feeling lonely and unfulfilled as my fundamental needs to be cared for, nurtured and loved were not being met and not just because he wouldn't or couldn't provide the things I needed. It was also a consequence of my own personal issues of being emotionally inhibited, not knowing how to ask for or receive the things I needed and because I harboured unconscious deep-seeded feelings of being undeserving. Both our underlying disorders acted together to co-create our dysfunction, our inherent feelings of inadequacy and unworthiness relentlessly drove us, albeit in different ways. My predominant character structure was masochistic/burdened enduring, his predominant character structure was psychopathic/narcissistic (refer to book 1). I was driven by the need to be self-sacrificing and he was driven by the need to be self-serving. My deeply held unconscious negative emotions were compensated for by being in service to others and seeking others approval, his deeply held unconscious negative emotions were compensated for by ignoring others needs and fulfilling his own.

The Beginning of the End

The last four years of my marriage were the darkest and most frightening period of my relationship as I was fighting for survival. My relationship resembled a battlefield and for me it became a constant series of strategies with the aim being to extricate myself and my children with the least possible damage. He was the aggressor and I was the defender I had no guidelines and so it was necessary to rely on my intellect and trust my intuition. My intention and ultimate goal, to free myself and my children from living under the same roof and under his control and to do it in a way that would permanently discourage him from coming after us. I desperately wanted to find and create a safe haven to live free from his oppressive nature, volatile temperament and the constant feeling of anxiety, fear and menace that he created. There were numerous times when I felt a sense of hopelessness and thought about giving up the fight as the battle was exhausting on all levels emotionally, psychologically and physically. The one constant that kept me looking to the future was the well-being of my children as I desperately wanted them to live in a healthy, happy and peaceful environment and I did not want them to grow up bearing the negative repercussions that would most certainly come if we stayed in this relationship. However, despite my exhaustive efforts it seemed to me that I wasn't making any headway. I had realised that this entire situation was beyond my limited experience, I needed to find a solution to free us that was not only safe but also permanent and I finally succumbed to the conclusion that I needed some sort of outside help.

My first step centred around the need to survive with my sanity intact, and so in order to do this I had to make sense of my life circumstances and the chaotic emotional roller coaster that I was experiencing. I knew I couldn't do it on my own but at the same time I felt it was vital to keep my secret, so my first natural inclination was to turn to books. I wanted and needed to understand myself and my abuser and had to try to make sense as to why this was happening. I was searching for answers to many questions such as, who is to blame? why did I end up in this dysfunctional relationship? how can I help myself? Should I stay or should I go? Can he change? Can I change? and many more. Fortunately, I possessed an innate thirst for knowledge and an enquiring mind, I was already a voracious reader and so I went on an emotional and psychological educational journey through books. Over time I read hundreds of books covering many diverse subjects from spirituality, philosophy, self-help, theology, inspirational and psychology.

On the first part of my journey with books I became intimately familiar with the word's "spirituality" and "metaphysics" and the understanding that perhaps there was something greater than the reality I was living and that there was more to my existence and more meaning to what I was experiencing. I spent quite some time exploring the many varying beliefs and teachings of philosophers, spiritual leaders and psychologists through authors such as Eckhart Tolle, Deepak Chopra, Marianne Williamson, Caroline Myss, Donald Walsch, Louise Hay, Doreen Virtue, Carl Jung, Sigmund Freud, Socrates (c. 469-399 B.C) and Rumi (1207-1273) to name just a few. To be quite honest I found some of the teachings to be contradictory and confusing and so I struggled with finding a possible singular belief system that I could completely trust to guide me to safe waters and hopefully peace and happiness. It's quite probable that my confusion had nothing to do with the teachings themselves but more likely with my own personal inexperience. I naively thought that if I were to thoroughly embrace one particular school of thought (ideology) I would be able to see myself comfortably through all of life's challenges.

Perhaps it was my own personal misunderstanding or interpretation of some of the philosophy, but instead of helping me some of the doctrine worked to hinder my progress in some areas of my life. For example, beliefs such as "to forgive is divine" or "forgive the person and not their actions", which both implied that by forgiving others who have harmed you is freeing and healing for you (the victim) and that the forgiveness itself is not based on the wrongdoer themselves but rather on their actions. This may be true in some cases, for some victims, and for a time I did embrace these concepts however it was to my personal detriment. Throughout our relationship I had forgiven my abuser many times, giving him numerous occasions to change his ways and ample opportunity to preserve our marriage and family unit. However, as it turned out it, it simply provided him with more time to continue to abuse us, prolonging the duration of his abuse. One of the beliefs that I cannot accept is the premise that if you forgive the abuser themselves and not their actions that you will find some personal relief or redemption. What a load of hogwash in my mind the abuser is "their actions" and there is no separating them. I tried very hard to forgive my abuser, but found it difficult and most often impossible when he continued to abuse me and my family. Although I didn't know it at the time, expecting him to change was a futile endeavour, it was never going to happen then or in the future, the fact remained that he was actually incapable of the changes that needed to happen. He did not possess the capacity for self-reflection, his psychological profile was such that it did not permit him to look at or question to closely, his actions.

Someone with a balanced psyche would possess the ability to reflect upon their own actions, leading to the possible tempering and/or questioning of negative behaviour, and with aid of a healthy dose of guilt, shame or remorse can change their thinking or correct their actions. For someone like my husband who was afflicted with a psychopathic /narcissistic character structure this is not possible as his narcissistic persona would have perceived self-reflection as an attempt to undermine the strength of his ego-identity. This leads to the total avoidance of self-reflection, the avoidance becomes a maladaptive and automatic defence that protects the ego-ideal he holds of himself and keeps unwanted feelings such as shame, guilt and remorse at bay. Remember tempering or questioning his behaviour would also interfere with his desire to satiate his needs, attain his goals and may call into question the integrity of his outwardly projected persona.

For the narcissistic abuser the identity they cling to and portray to the world is of critical importance to their psychological and emotional stability. They will never cope with a threat to what they believe to be their personal or professional integrity or accept a fall from grace in the eyes of their family, friends or co-workers. They will go to great lengths to restore their standing or to maintain the façade that they have created and will likely retaliate if it is challenged in any significant way. This was the case with my abuser, he could not tolerate his family, friends, co-workers and business associates ever thinking of him other than that which he portrayed to them. He was perceived as being a great friend to his mates, a savvy business man and a steadfast family provider, even though those who were closest to him knew he could be demanding, stubborn and selfish at times. For the most part however, they experienced him as a "man's man", a sports buff who possessed a larger-than-life persona. He was known to be quick-witted, humorous, confident and gregarious which made it difficult even for those closest to him to ever perceive or believe that there existed an abuser lurking beneath the surface of the facade.

My abuser's behaviour in the last seven years of our marriage escalated as he spent more and more time indulging his whims and desires while trying to keep his fears at bay. He had a serious health scare at the age of thirty-eight, he was diagnosed with sleep apnoea and critical high blood pressure due to a weight problem, he was also a heavy smoker and drinker. This diagnosis prompted a campaign by him to lose weight and improve his health and fitness, which he did achieve over the next year, however during the interim he was a nightmare to live with as I was blamed and then punished for his self-induced health issues. It was around the time when we were both nearing the age of forty years old when things seemed to get worse as his behaviour was becoming more erratic, mid-life was edging in and he was not coping well with leaving his youth behind.

He became conspicuously absent for most of the week, his weekends included playing golf or going to football games and then drinks with the boys, his weekdays included attending social or business lunches and dinners including Friday night drinks with the boys, while I was kept busy rearing our children and taking care of our home. I had spoken with a couple of my most intimate girlfriends about his erratic behaviour, as it was also becoming noticeable by close family and friends, in particular by his mates. He could not stay in any one place for long before he made excuses and disappeared, it was impossible to keep track of where he was. We all came to the conclusion that he was suffering a "mid-life crisis" and that he was depressed and anxious as a result and so our collective solution was to indulge him, thinking that he was going through a phase and would soon get over it and settle down. This however was in part the truth as he seemed to appear to be going through what may be termed as a "mid-life crisis", better known as a "fear of aging" or an attempt to cling to one's youth.

However, upon reflection I believe he was in actuality, unconsciously being driven by what is known in psychology as "Peter Pan Syndrome" (refer to kingdom of wolves' book one). This is a term used to describe someone who is trapped in "never, never land" (their youth or teenage years), wherein they are emotionally and psychologically impaired and do not wholly mature into adulthood. This was true of my husband who was desperately trying to cling to his youth and as a result sought ways in which to fortify feeling young and omnipotent over and over again. One way in which he achieved this was through sexual encounters with women outside the marriage, sometimes it was with paid prostitutes and other times it was with random women he had picked up at the bars he frequented.

At that time, it had crossed my mind that he might be having extra-marital sex but I dismissed those fleeting thoughts because I could not equate the man that so earnestly wanted to stay married to me as someone who would jeopardise it with an affair or one-night stand. Despite our dysfunction and his abusive behaviour, I really thought we loved each other and it was consistently implied to me by him that we were a tight unit that nothing could derail. I was under the delusion that he would never be disloyal to me or cheat on our marriage because we had an active sex life, I naively mistook this to mean that we shared an unspoken intimate and sacred bond. He on the other hand did not, it was many years later that I had realised that he had been unfaithful from the start of our relationship through to the end of our relationship. His need to be promiscuous was driven by his need to feel youthful, powerful and in control, hence the need to consistently prove his virility. So, what I thought of as his mid-life crisis was in fact part of his narcissistic disorder that supported his serial promiscuity to which he became addicted. The worst part about this is not just the betrayal of fidelity and all the emotional fallout that comes with that, but that he had through his immaturity, selfishness and thoughtlessness continuously put my health and wellbeing at risk as well as our children's.

He never used protection (condoms) with women he entered into a continued relationship with, leaving the responsibility of birth control to them as he did with me. In his over-confident, narcissistic mind he assumed that the women he had a relationship with would without doubt remain monogamous to him (therefore disease risk free) simply because he would have expected it. Especially if he's footing the bill for them and also because he would have thought that they had to be completely satisfied (not want or need anyone else) with his sexual prowess. He consistently, egotistically underestimated or overestimated women based on his limited relationship experience, assuming that if he could deceive his wife and all of the other women in his life (mother, sister, female relatives and wives of friends) with his charming, manipulations than all women could be coerced, misled and controlled. His negligence, stupidity and ignorance exposed itself when he entered into a long-term relationship with a young woman, he met randomly at a bar. She was a part-time prostitute but had "apparently" stopped her so-called side-line when they "hooked up" together. He had helped set her up in an apartment and had supported her financially for a time assuming that this guaranteed her faithfulness and loyalty to him.

However, unfortunately as it turned out she had ended up with a mild venereal disease and as a result of course I had to get tested. I was cleared luckily, and this is when I found out that he had not used protection and never had throughout his relationship with her, during this discussion I discovered that it had never occurred to him that she could possibly have been promiscuous. I knew this because when I suggested it to him, he looked at me with an incredulous expression on his face while he was weighing up the probability of my conjecture, it was then that the penny had finally dropped for him, I could visibly see the change in face as realisation dawned. The fact is that I knew and he knew that I had not been promiscuous and so that left only two other possible transgressors of infidelity in his relationship with her, either himself or his mistress. I was outraged at his negligence, thoughtlessness, and selfishness, it never occurred to him that if I was at risk of a venereal disease than I was also at risk of more serious life-threatening health consequences such as hepatitis, Aids and/or HIV and consequently so were our children.

This incident highlighted his immature, self-absorbed nature, and his predisposition to self-indulge without thought or care of the consequences. Unfortunately, this was the second time I had to get tested, the first time was when I found out about the affair. It was both anxiety provoking and humiliating for me to go to my doctor again and run the gamut of blood tests then wait the three months to be completely cleared of infection. I confided in my doctor as to the reasons I needed the blood tests again, she was the epitome of professionality and extremely understanding and empathetic, however this did not make the process any easier to do. This entire incident, the health scare, the doctor's visit, and the three-month waiting period afterward was more unnecessary trauma I had to undergo and an added layer of concern to my list of fears and worries.

The Broken Bed

His affair with this woman was the one that I discovered, a fortuitous blessing in many ways as it was the catalyst that marked the domino of events that inspired the beginning of the end of our unsound relationship. There are distinct red flags that alert a person to the possibility that their partner is having sexual relations outside of their relationship and of course without their knowledge, however I unfortunately was one of those people who was too inexperienced to be aware of them. I was responsible for and absorbed by the running our home, working, cultivating and sustaining our social life and later rearing our children all the while operating under the assumption that we were both working towards and wanted the same things. I placed my entire naïve faith in the strength of what I believed to be a shared intimate bond between us, trusting that like myself he would remain faithful. I was possessed with a kind of blind loyalty that never wavered, I wanted to and needed to believe in our relationship as I had projected all my hopes for happiness in our future together.

However, this all changed when his unusual behaviours became increasingly noticeably obvious and persistent, and his lies more inconsistent. It was the accumulation of these odd behaviours that became impossible for me to disregard, forcing me in a sense to sit up and take note. I started to become aware of strange behaviours, such as when his mobile phone rang, he would take the call and walk away from me whether we were in a private or a social setting. He changed the access code to his phone keeping his phone calls and messages inaccessible, when I questioned him about this, he said it was in case his phone was stolen and for business privacy reasons and refused to elaborate further. There were also occasions when I could not contact him and so I would leave repeated messages until he replied, forcing him to answer, to which he would either text a reply telling me he will call me later or return my call and talk in whisper quiet tones, citing that he was in an important meeting.

His other behaviours included being absent from home for even longer periods of time than was usual for him and at the same time never answering my text messages or phone calls enquiring after his whereabouts but rather always calling me back when he was in his car. He would explain this behaviour by saying that he was in a business meeting, or his phone was off, or that his phone was on silent and he had forgotten to change the setting from silent. Sometimes he came home in a good mood, making him more pleasant to be around, but more often than not he came home tired and extremely moody and so I did not want to antagonise him further or ignite one of his rages. I noticed that he started meeting up more often with particular acquaintances that I was not all that familiar with or with random associates from his work, this of course made it impossible for me to verify his whereabouts. The biggest problem he had was keeping his lies straight, his explanations were a compilation of illogical and convoluted rationalisations and half-truths that inflamed my suspicions. He realised that I was noticing his odd and extreme behaviours and that I was now seriously questioning the validity of his excuses. In order to counteract my enquires, he would go into attack mode, challenging every question I asked concerning his whereabouts by steadfastly refuting any wrongdoing with righteous indignation. He had a habit of discrediting and invalidating my arguments thereby sidelining the original and actual enquiry or he would accuse me of being neurotic, irrational and/or paranoid particularly if I pointed out an inconsistency in his story.

There were two particular ways he tended to operate, the first being he believed that to "attack is the best mode of defence," by doing this he was always able to derail the trajectory of the conversation, instead of it being about him it would become about me or our relationship and the issue of trust. His other favoured mode of operating was to use psychological manipulation through the act of "gaslighting," his intention was to undermine and manipulate my quest for the truth. This method of operation is commonly used by many abusers, their aim is to redefine the reality or truth of a situation to suit the one wanting the change (the abuser) and at the same time forcing the one it is projected onto (the victim) to question themselves, their version of the facts and their own reality. Long term use of this type of abuse on a victim creates extreme emotional instability and can cause them to become anxiety ridden, depressed, self-conscious, indecisive, mistrustful and disorientated. Most will lose their self-confidence and self-worth questioning their every thought and action and some may even believe they are going insane.

He had repeatedly used this type of manipulation throughout our relationship, causing me to think that I was losing my sanity, because the incongruencies in his stories kept playing over and over in my mind no matter how hard I tried to make sense of them. This was torturous as I was continuously emotionally and mentally conflicted, I had my version of events which was what I actually thought and felt and what logic was telling me was true and yet he was refusing to accept, acknowledge or admit anything contrary to his version of events. He was relentless in his arguments changing the facts around until he found a possible weakness on my part and then he would pounce on and exploit this weakness. This worked for him for a long time because he was clever enough to have used a small element of the truth in every story to support the bigger untruth he was actually perpetrating. For example, he would tell me he was going to meet an old friend for dinner, someone I knew but was not close to, then he would meet this friend for a quick dinner followed by an assignation with whichever female he was seeing at the time. Hence there was a small kernel of truth to the majority of the stories he told, he made this small fact the focus, knowing that I could not call this acquaintance to verify whether he was telling the truth or not.

He spent years gaslighting me until I lost all confidence in my intuition, questioning myself and my thoughts multiple times when things didn't add up, rather than focusing on the validity of his actions and assertions. However, this took an about face one day when while reading an article on adultery I came across the axiom "if you have nothing to hide, you hide nothing". This saying had a profound effect on me because it made me really truly reflect on my husband's secrecy and disinformation, it acted as a catalyst causing me to re-evaluate the way I was approaching this situation. I had decided it was time to stop questioning his actions and torturing myself with the resulting conflicting emotions and thoughts. I needed to go on a fact-finding mission for sanities sake and so that he could no longer accuse me of being neurotic, paranoid and irrational and he would be unable to deny the truth. It felt incredibly personally empowering to become pro-active about the situation, providing me with an unexpected feeling of strength. I wasn't sure where this was going to lead but I felt compelled to search for the truth, I desperately needed answers. I was split in two, on the one hand I wanted to find out that he was indeed having an affair, because then I would finally receive the validation that the conflicting thoughts and feelings, I was experiencing were in fact true and I was not going crazy. Which would go a long way to restoring my personal power and provide me with some leverage in our relationship, something I had never experienced with him before. On the other hand, I did not know how I would cope when I found out the truth, because it meant that everything, I thought I had with him was not real, which felt as if it would be devastating for me. I knew it would be incredibly difficult to cope with the blow to my fragile self-esteem and it would also likely trigger my deeply held feelings of failure and unworthiness.

However, despite my trepidation and even though I was split by opposing thoughts and feelings, that part of me that needed to know, was driven to find the truth. I felt compelled to forge ahead, not knowing that this new journey was the start of an unexpected reformation for me. I started with the small things like scrutinising our shared visa card bill to look at what he was purchasing and to see if I could find a pattern of where he was buying his petrol. I would, when it was possible physically check the facts by going to some of the places where he said he was going to be or I would randomly drive past his work or gym and check that his car was there. This lasted months, until one day he came home to tell me he was going on a boys golfing weekend to Hobart in Tasmania with a couple of work associates that I did not know. From the moment he announced his plans my body responded with angst, something did not ring true but I could do nothing about it. In the days leading up to his weekend getaway, he was behaving strangely out of character causing me to become suspicious, he was acting overly agreeable and cheerful towards me and our children. The night before he was due to leave was when my mind and body went into high-alert, he was exhibiting signs of nervous excitement and he was paying me undue attention, something he had never displayed before especially if he was just going on a boy's weekend away. The dead give-away that something was definitely amiss, was that he gave me some cash a few hundred dollars and told me to spend it on myself. The problem with this was that he had never done this before as he was often tight-fisted with our money where frivolity was concerned and so this sudden display of generosity could only mean one thing and that was that he was trying to cover-up and/or compensate for some type of misconduct that he was committing.

He left early the next morning to catch his flight, and as soon as I dropped the kids to school, I came home and started searching for information to prove or disprove my disquieting feelings and thoughts. First step, telephone our visa card provider and ask for the payment of flight details as his card belonged to a joint account, it was relatively easy for me to get the information I was seeking. He was travelling with another person; someone I did not know and I was not sure if it was a male or female because both the first and second names could be interpreted as being unisex. The next step I decided to take was to call his place of accommodation in Hobart to enquire after the identity of the person he was travelling with. This required careful thought, it had to be discreet so as reception did not alert him to my enquiry and I also had to find a way that allowed me to breach the privacy protocol that hotels usually adhere to. This I achieved by pretending to be his personal assistant calling to confirm whether he and his partner had arrived at the hotel because his work colleagues and I wanted to organise a gift hamper delivered to his room for his anniversary.

The receptionist confirmed that he had indeed arrived and was booked into one of the hotels finest suites with his wife, to which I politely thanked her and told her I would call back with the delivery details. I was a mix of emotions at first, I was shocked and doubted what I had heard, however the conversation repeatedly played itself over and over in my mind until I came to the conclusion that what I heard must be true and then I felt devastated. This was quickly followed by burgeoning anger, gradually morphing into unmitigated rage towards him, I started to replay in my mind not just recent events and the fact that he made me question my sanity and accused me of being neurotic but the entirety of our lives together. This included every abusive event that had been perpetrated on me and the brutality, callousness, and selfishness with which I was treated. I thought about the lack of support and the feelings of loneliness, neglect, and abandonment that I had experienced throughout our relationship. I felt like an absolute fool who had been used and discarded and sadly my self-esteem and self-worth plummeted to new levels of low. I never envisaged I would experience the tumult of emotions that assailed me as a result of this one phone conversation.

I struggled with these emotions for most of the day and was unable to contain them so I called one of our closest friends, someone my husband and I both trusted, he was more mature than many of our other friends and not given to drama or hysterics. I knew he would have both our best interests at heart. I explained what had occurred and stated that I still held some doubts about what I had heard, but that I was strongly contemplating flying over to check the facts for myself. He supported me in my endeavour saying that the only way I would ever be able to find a resolution was to go there and see for myself and if he was there by chance with a golfing mate then I could tell him I joined him there as a surprise. However, if he was there with a woman then I would have my answer as to his fidelity and the situation would be resolved either way. I made the decision to fly to Hobart and find out one way or the other, and so I drove to the shopping mall to book my flight. I was there for over three hours walking around, drinking copious amounts of coffee and smoking cigarettes until I worked up the courage to book a flight, I struggled with doubt while my emotions hovered between rage, anxiety and fear. I ruminated about all the possible scenarios that could occur as a result of what I am about to do, replaying them over and over in my mind, the most significant being that I was afraid of what his reaction would be if I had got it all wrong and he was actually there with a golfing buddy. I finally overcame my fears and booked a flight and a motel that was just down the road from the landmark hotel he was staying at, I was to leave early that very evening. I organised last minute baby-sitting for my children, packed a bag and flew over, I was not only terrified of what might happen when I confronted him but I was not a good flyer to begin with and it was pouring with rain when I left Melbourne.

I arrived at the motel and something felt off in my body, it just didn't feel right to stay there, it had an eerie kind of "psycho motel" vibe to it and as I was walking to my room, I received a call from the friend I had confided in. He happened to be in an office with a mutual acquaintance, a female friend, who coincidently had just separated from her philandering husband. She advised me not to stay there if I was uncomfortable, the only other hotel available at short notice was the one my husband was staying at, and so she proceeded to book a room for me using a fake name, saying I was one of her sales representatives. So as fate would have it, I was destined to complete what I had set out to do making my way to the hotel with great trepidation, wandering if I would run into him in the foyer and dreading it. I was very familiar with the hotel lay-out as I had stayed there twice before with him, I knew that there was a small bar situated right near the foyer that we had spent much time in during our previous stays. I arrived and was standing at the reception counter trying to make myself as small and unobtrusive as possible, hoping I could speed up my booking and get the hell out of the foyer.

Then two astonishing things happened simultaneously, firstly I had an epiphany of sorts a sudden inspiration that compelled me not to use the pseudonym I was so graciously provided with by my friend's acquaintance but that I should use my real name. This was followed by a story that just flowed from my lips, I'm not even sure how in the midst of all the heightened emotion I was experiencing that I came up with this particular verbal narrative. I stated that I had just flown into Hobart to surprise my brother whom I had not seen for several years as I had been living and working overseas. I asked them not to tell him that I was here and that I would like to surprise him and his wife in person and asked if I could have his room number. The staff at the counter were titillated with the whole idea, and so they confirmed that he was indeed staying with his wife and graciously provided me his room number.

The second astonishing albeit highly alarming event that occurred while I was standing at the counter anxiously waiting for my room-key and a porter. I was furtively taking surreptitious glances to the left and right, trying to keep a lookout for my nemesis, when to my shock and dismay I spot him and freeze. There he is sitting on a bar stool, somewhat camouflaged by the latticed screening surrounding the bar, I knew without a doubt that it was him, he was tossing back a drink not twenty metres from where I was standing. I could not see who was sitting next to him and I was almost hyperventilating from anxiousness, while I was chanting in my head for the staff to hurry the f**k up. I knew that if he saw me now that I would never get the opportunity to catch him unaware and it would render all my efforts redundant and there was also the possibility that he could react badly to my even being there in the first place, lucky for me I was safely ensconced in my room before being exposed.

Within minutes of settling into my room, I was surprised to find myself experiencing a deep and utter calmness, it enveloped me like a warm blanket on a cold night relieving me of my anxiety and fear and providing me with clarity of thought. It was a profoundly cathartic moment and I knew intrinsically that I was right where I should be in this moment in time and for the first time in a long time I felt as if I was aligned in mind, body and instinct. I was experiencing a strange feeling of oneness, my thoughts and emotions though heightened in alertness were also clear and stable, rather than my usual feelings of disconnectedness, instability and apprehension. For most of my life these negative and debilitating emotions ruled me, making me feel as if I was treading in deep water, fighting for my physical, emotional and psychological survival. It suddenly occurred to me that I had not been in the flow of life instead I have persistently resisted my natural inclinations and instincts until I lost my trust in them and in turn ultimately severing my connection to my authenticity. Through the act of overcoming my trepidation enough to listen to and respect my intuition, I had enabled myself to become reacquainted with my own innate inner wisdom. It was guiding me towards the truth and wholeness, reminding me of the strength and sense of peace that lies within reach when one is in unity of mind, body and instinct.

In order to catch my husband unaware, I needed a plan that would allow me enter into his suite at the very last minute. From personal experience I presumed that he would be out drinking and gambling through to the early hours of the morning and so I decided that I would wait until three or four am before going to his suite to confront him. My instinct also told me that if he saw me through the peep hole in his door that he would never voluntarily allow me entry into his suite. He would either not answer the door or he would subvert the situation by removing me from the scene with some excuse until he could relocate her. I could not let that happen as it would render all my efforts thus far for naught and it would make him doubly cautious in the future. I decided on a plan of action that I hoped would give me the greatest chance of success which entailed me waiting until the early hours of the following day. At precisely 3.45am the next morning I ordered the best bottle of champagne that the hotel had to offer, it was delivered to my room on a trolley along with a porter. That porter didn't know it but he was about to become an integral instrument in my deception. I told him the very same story I had used on the hotel reception staff of wanting to surprise my brother and his wife after an extended stay overseas and asked if would be happy to accompany me to my "brothers" suite, which he was thrilled to do. I planned for the waiter to knock on my husband's door, while I stood to the side out of view, he was to tell my "my brother" (husband) that the hotel was providing a complimentary bottle of champagne. I knew this manoeuvre would play into my husbands over inflated ego, he readily accepted the "hotel gift" never taking into account the abnormality of the hour in which it was being delivered. My strategy worked, and as the porter made his way down the short hallway entrance, I stepped in right behind him following him into the suite.

This was the first time I had ever rendered my husband speechless; he was shocked and I noticed that his face was slowly leeching of colour as his blood flow was steadily heading south. The porter realised that something was not right, he stood stock still not knowing how to proceed, however the light must have dawned when I told him that we wouldn't be needing his services or the bottle of champagne anymore and asked him politely to return the bottle to housekeeping. After the porter left, I broke the silence by congratulating him on his choice of suite, it was stately compared to the small rooms we had occupied on our previous stays at this hotel. I followed this by opening the drapes that blocked out the majestic view of the river that the room overlooked, remarking on the beautiful vista. When I turned around my husband was still standing there motionless in his underwear and I imagine completely shaken. I walked to the king-size bed that dominated the suite to see who this woman was and to take her measure, the young woman looking back at me was clearly shocked by my sudden appearance. Neither of us uttered a word, though I could see she was extremely uncomfortable, time seemed to stand still while we took each other in, it was probably only a minute or so but it seemed longer, she then hastily made some excuse and quickly retreated to the bathroom.

By this stage my husband had regained some of his composure, putting on some clothes and babbling out an apology, I was not interested in what he had to say and told him not to concern himself with my wellbeing. I suggested that he stay on and complete his holiday, however when he did get back, he needed to look for a new place to live. He pleaded to speak to me in private knowing I was leaving shortly to go to the airport, I acquiesced giving him my room number and within minutes he came to speak to me. He proceeded to tell me that this was a one-time weekend fling, that he had never done this before and would never do it again, this was followed by a barrage of excuses, denials and minimisations concerning his behaviour. This was also accompanied with proclamations of his deep and abiding love for me, our children and our life together.

He didn't ask for my forgiveness but rather persistently declared he was sorry and even managed to squeeze out a few tears. I also shed my fair share of tears that day however, I was resolute when I told him that he needn't rush back to Melbourne, and that I would personally pack his belongings to be ready for him to pick up when he returned home. On the flight home I had time to reflect over the scenes of the drama that had unfolded, however, my thoughts kept circling back to the young woman who until now was an unknown person to me. I wondered who she was, why she was with this older and controlling man, was she looking for an easy ride no strings attached or did she imagine a future with my husband. Prior to sighting her, I had credited many exaggerated attributes to this supposed "scarlet" woman imagining that she was someone younger, slim, very pretty if not beautiful, well endowed (he was a boob man), tall with dark hair (I was a blonde). Well, the reality was that yes, she was taller than me by three or four inches and yes, she was younger than me by twenty-four years but she was not the bombshell my wounded ego had envisaged. In fact, upon sighting her I realised almost immediately that she was just as much a victim as I was, even though I was not yet aware of the circumstances that connected her to my husband. She wasn't that much older than our daughter was at the time and I can remember thinking that irrespective of her relationship with my husband, my beef was not with her and that the culpability for this affair solely rests on his shoulders alone. I was not married to her, I was married to him, it was his responsibility to his wife and family to remain loyal, loving and trustworthy not hers. Don't misunderstand me I did not harbour any undue sympathy for her but I could understand how someone at that age could easily be misled and it didn't really matter who she was, it was my partner who went looking for someone to have an affair or tryst with.

I knew better than anyone that my husband was a prolific liar, a manipulator and a narcissist, he thought that he could keep his two worlds from colliding forever. After he returned to Melbourne, he professed his deep and enduring love for me, he pleaded with me to give our relationship another try with promises that this would never happen again etc. etc. I didn't believe him but for the sake of our children I decided I would give him an opportunity to make good. He told me he would never contact or see this young woman again and he completely changed his behaviour and demeanour, he became considerate and attentive to me and the children. I was cautiously optimistic, however as was true to form for him, his good intentions and promises lasted about two weeks before it all started again. My "deceit radar" (instinct) was ignited again and just like before, I was conflicted with the issue of what was true and what was not, something was not right even though he was staying in contact with me letting me know where he was most of the time. This is when the crazed part of me came out, I decided to investigate his every movement to check the validity of his whereabouts. I scrutinised his visa card and telephone bills, I would look for anything that I might consider to be an odd purchase and I would study the pattern of his petrol purchases. I could not sit back and wait for him to make a blatant mistake, I had to know that he was where he said he was going to be, so I would drive to his professed whereabouts to verify that he was indeed there, this was not always possible with two young children but I managed for the most part. I was a nut-case speeding from one place to another around Melbourne like a lunatic, it was supremely personally distressing that I had reduced myself to this state of madness.

One of the biggest fallouts from the affair was that the trust in our relationship was destroyed, possibly irretrievably and it meant that it would require that there be significant changes in how we operated as a couple. Before the affair I trusted him, he could go anywhere, see anybody at any time, I never questioned his loyalty and fidelity and he was likewise the same with me, this was no longer the case for obvious reasons. The other major issue that caused much contention between us was that I was obsessed with wanting to know every detail about the affair, where he met her, how long has it been going on, why did he do it, was this reflection on our sex life, where were the places they frequented, who knows about her etc. etc. This subject was hashed and re-hashed as his answers did not satisfy my curiosity, appease my insecurities or calm my anxieties they were generic, uncomplicated answers that appeared rehearsed and lacked real sincerity. Our bedroom ironically took centre stage for all our hushed discussions at night and our outright arguments and fights. It was during one of these discussions and based on naught but my own discernment, that I had accused him of having had sex with his girlfriend on our marital bed. He vehemently denied any such wrongdoing, expressing a deep indignation at the very idea and accused me of being neurotic. However, I knew different, call it intuition but I would not accept his denial, I just wanted some truth to come out of his mouth and so while we were yelling at each other he sat down on the bed in a huff and the bed collapsed. Our bed was broken, it took us both by surprise as this was a solid mahogany sleigh bed not something easily damaged, I took this to be a symbolic reflection of our fractured and likely irreparable relationship and a sign or a message that he was indeed lying to me.

Lies, Lies and More Lies

I became obsessed with catching him in a lie, this became my daily ritual, I would drop the kids off to school followed by picking up a large coffee on my way home. I lived on a steady diet of coffee and cigarettes and very little nutritious food or drink, I lost my appetite, so by the time this lunacy ended I was half my body weight and besieged with illnesses. My days consisted of very quickly rushing through my home duties and then I would pour all my energy into research and reconnaissance (that may or may not have involved a bit of stalking). The first clue I worked on was using the young woman's name that I had procured from my husband's original visa card bill wherein he had paid for her airfare to Tasmania. I looked up the addresses of all persons with the first initial and second name like hers and then I cross-referenced it to the suburbs where I found my husband had recently bought petrol that fell out of his normal routes. Then bingo, I narrowed it down to what I thought had to be her address, I spent the next two or three weeks surveilling this home, just patiently waiting to catch a glimpse of her or my husband. However, I never did sight either of them there, much to my chagrin because I was actually stalking the wrong address, something I found out a little later on. This foolhardy and embarrassing escapade was effectively a waste of time and energy and my behaviour drew some very uncomfortable attention from the neighbours to this property who began to take note of my presence.

This failed escapade did not deter me for long, it prompted me to move my surveillance to another location which was still in the same area, however this time I was going to stay close to the petrol station that I noticed he frequented. This was to be the site of a rather bizarre incident, one that upon reflection could be viewed as comical, but at the time was actually dangerous and had the potential of being personally harmful to me. It happened on a lovely spring morning, I was parked in a side street it was mid-morning, the sun was shining, I cranked open my driver's side window and the passenger side window about two or three inches to let the warm breeze flow through. I then reclined my driver's seat back slightly and closed my eyes while contemplating what in the hell I was doing here, this was crazy, I am nuts, I used to be level headed, sane and logical or so I thought. I was probably there for approximately fifteen or twenty minutes, when suddenly a large shadow loomed blocking the light from the passenger side window. This broke my quiet reverie; I immediately opened my eyes and to my horror a rather large man was desperately trying to open the passenger side door.

He appeared dishevelled and harried and his fingers had latched onto the window in a vice-like grip, his knuckles were white and he was repeatedly asking me to let him into the car while looking over his shoulder. He had a New Zealand accent and the looks and size of a Māori, he was terrifying, in the meantime my eyes were glued to him while my hands were frantically trying to find the electric window button. I don't remember if I said anything because it all happened so quickly, he then took one more look to his right and took off running, I noticed that he had one pant leg rolled up and a bloody shin. This was my cue to start the engine and get the hell out of dodge and as I was about to take off, a car drives past me with four rather large looking men inside, they noted me but kept going after the guy who took off running. I immediately slid the car into drive and hit the accelerator. However instead of driving straight home I drove round the corner to a public car-lot which was adjacent to the petrol station I had been surveilling and immediately parked my car. My heart was racing, my hands were shaking, I needed a couple of minutes to calm down and gather my thoughts and as soon as I caught my breath, I took note of my surroundings and noticed that the parking lot was deserted.

As I am about to reverse out and head home, I catch sight of an old white beat-up minivan it was moving directly towards me blocking me from reversing out of my spot and it stood between me and the exit. The van stopped and the two rough looking men in the front seat eyeballed me and my car and then slowly drove away. It was like a scene from a Guy Ritchie movie, I immediately drove home berating myself about the dangers of stalking and promising myself that I would never engage in that behaviour again. I realised through this experience that my behaviour was bordering on the ridiculous and that this stalking had to stop and it did. It was time for me to hire a private investigator to hand the stalking over to the professionals, and by accident or you could say good fortune, I happened to come across one while I was visiting a medical specialist in a high-rise office building around the corner from my home. Despite my trepidation and some concern about their ability to be successful and discreet, I hired a private investigating team, who three days later followed my husband on a "supposed" dinner date he had planned with a friend. They followed his every movement from the moment he left home, they collected video footage of him picking up a female, kissing her in the front seat of the car, then having dinner with her and they followed him as he took her home, and then filmed him entering her apartment, in which he stayed for the next two hours. While this was happening, I was at home, I went through the usual nightly rituals with my children and then got them off to bed all the while battling anxiety, self-doubt and fear. My biggest two fears were that the private investigating team following him would expose themselves to him and that he would become enraged at them and then figure out it was me who hired them or that on this particular occasion my husband really was just having dinner with a male friend rendering all my efforts futile.

The private investigator called me on his way home to report his findings and to say he was sorry that he was the bearer of bad news, I was to pick up a copy of the DVD the next day. I asked him to describe the woman and when he did, I realised who it was. As it turned out, I was right all along, my husband had either re-kindled his affair with the woman from Tasmania or he had never ended it when he said he had, I was inclined towards believing the latter. After I hung up from the private investigator, I called him and as per usual he didn't answer, so I left a message for him to call me. As the minutes ticked by, I was very slowly but surely becoming furious and so I called him multiple times leaving repeated messages on his phone telling him to call me and then on the last call I left him this message "I know where you are, don't bother coming home". Within minutes of this last call, he returned my call and I could hear him getting in and starting his car, asking me what I was talking about. I proceeded to inform him of the information that was disclosed to me by the private investigator. He denied everything and said he was coming home immediately and that I needed to calm down, to which I responded by hanging up on him. I then grabbed a duffle bag, threw in some of his belongings, tossed it out onto the front porch and waited for him to arrive.

When he arrived, I told him that no explanations were necessary, we are over and that he needed to look for a new place to live. He was still trying to deny that there was any truth to what I had discovered and so I revealed to him that I had private investigators follow him and they had collected video footage of his activities. He was so astounded that I had truly hired someone to follow him that he was rendered speechless, as always, he had underestimated my tenacity and ingenuity. We talked all night into the early hours of the morning but only because he would not leave the premises, forcing his way past me into our home. He wanted to persuade me into believing that what I was going to see on the video was not what it implied, this was an innocent catch-up between himself and his supposed ex-lover. The only way I could make him stop brow-beating me was to promise to let him see the video footage and allow him the opportunity to explain his side of the story.

I gave in to his demand to see the footage so that I could make him stop and leave me alone, I was exhausted, hurt and in need of some respite. The next afternoon we both watched the footage in silence, he responded with a ridiculous explanation. According to him, this was going to be the very last time he was to see her, he believed he owed it to her to help her find employment as he had withdrawn his financial support. The dinner was his way of saying goodbye, and when he kissed her hello, it was purely out of habit, it meant nothing. He further explained that going up to her apartment for the two or so hours after dinner was to help her to compose a "resumé" for a job interview she had coming up. He argued that because the private investigators did not retrieve footage of what occurred after he went into the apartment then there was no proof of any infidelity occurring. It was of little consequence to him that he was again betraying my trust by lying about who he was with and his whereabouts. He profusely apologised for his actions, I didn't believe one word that came out of his mouth and told him so, but he was determined to stick to this preposterous fabrication.

He further insisted that he was not leaving our family home and that he was going to prove to me that my doubts were unfounded even if I did not want him to. The thing is, he didn't understand that whether or not he committed an act of infidelity that night he still lied to me about his whereabouts, who he was with and what he was doing which he considered to be a minor, forgivable bit of misconduct. I know at this stage you might be asking the question, why didn't I and my children leave as soon as the opportunity presented itself. The answer to that is that he would not let us, please remember he was a bully who would resort to coercion and/or violence to resolve his issues, there was no way he was going to let us just walk out the door and he said as much. Once again, I was forced to accept his relationship restorative efforts, even though by this stage I had already mentally and emotionally checked out of our marriage and I detested everything about him.

Within a few short weeks of declaring his love and fidelity to me, his behaviour became suspicious again, drawing us both into the next drama. With this incident I decided to plant a miniature tape recorder in his car before he went out for a prearranged dinner engagement with a supposed "old friend". The following morning after his dinner assignation, while he was in the shower, I retrieved the planted tape-recorder; however, I could not bring myself to listen to the contents until many days later. I needed time to prepare myself, I was as usual plagued with feelings of self-doubt, anxiety and a level of shame and guilt at how I had gone about retrieving the information. Contrary to what some of you may think, whether you believe my actions to be justified or not, the truth is all this subterfuge did not sit well with me, despite the fact that he was consistently committing acts of duplicity.

When I did finally find the courage to listen to the tape, I was deeply hurt by what I heard, it was a series of intimate conversations between two people who were clearly affectionate with each other, and who were also undoubtedly in a sexual relationship as evidenced by the contents. The contents could not be denied or glossed over; the subject matter indicated that this was the same woman he had said he had stopped seeing. Here we are again, both pulled into the vortex of the drama that is inherent in his life and to which the rest of us, myself and our children have to involuntarily participate. I called him at work to tell him about the tape recording, he came home immediately demanding access to the tape recorder, I denied him access but recited to him some of the contents which rendered him mute. We were both disconcertingly calm throughout our discussion over the tape-recording, he told me he found it hard to believe that I could do something like this, to which I responded with the statement that he always underestimates my resolve and ability to find the truth.

He was determined to get his hands on the tape-recorder and he harassed me daily for the next week until I relented and gave it to him. He took it away to listen to privately and then called me back to give me what I thought was the first and only heart-felt apology that I had heard from him in years, however it did not impact or in any way lessen the degree of pain caused by yet another betrayal despite my contentious feelings towards him. We entered into a strange impasse, I asked him to leave our home and requested a divorce, he refused and became resolutely determined to re-establish our relationship. There was no deterring him from his intention and because of his volatile nature and abusive predilection, I was forced to concede to his restorative efforts yet again. He could not envisage a life without me and the children in it and decided we were not leaving him or our home and set about forcing this to happen. As far as I was concerned, we were done, I could not take anymore and I needed him out of my and my children's life, I wanted to be free from the anxiety and turmoil that he continued to create and I wanted peace from the constant drama that accompanied his life's antics. Our sexual relationship had ended, I asked him to sleep on the couch, he refused to do so, he likely thought that if we shared a bed, he would better persuade me back into an intimate relationship with him. This was never going to happen as far as I was concerned, I slept on the couch and I did this for the next eighteen months without my children ever finding out, I was up at the crack of dawn every day removing all evidence of my bedding.

The Revelation

It seems that universally women and men who have been victims of adultery by a cheating partner invariably envisage the adulterer's partner in crime to be more attractive than they are or at least to be special in some way. This helps to fortify a victim's low self-esteem, thinking that it would have to be someone more than ordinary (perhaps in their sexuality, personality or looks) that captures the attention of their philandering partner. However, in reality this is not often the case, ordinary people have affairs with other ordinary people and the attraction does not necessarily have anything to do with their appearance, personality or sexual nature but rather more to do with the philanderer's own immaturity and low self-esteem. Regardless of the reason for the affair, it still has a profound deflating effect on a victim's confidence. In my case, my existing low self-esteem hit an all-time low, I could not help but compare myself to the young woman my husband had the affair with even though I knew nothing about her. This was ridiculous, self-defeating behaviour that was typical of my underlying masochistic/burdened enduring character structure (refer to character structure book one). I was like many victims of infidelity in the sense that instead of placing the totality of the feelings of shame, inadequacy and failure that invariably arise from an act of infidelity where they belong, solely with the philanderer, I internalised them in part myself.

Affairs are not about a victim's deficiencies, they are about the cheater's deficiencies, however when something like this happens there is an inevitable process that occurs for both the victim and the perpetrator that no one can foresee, are prepared for, or can control. I did not anticipate that I would ever feel the way I did when I finally found out about my husband's promiscuity. Thinking my partner was having an affair was quite different to the reality of finding out he was actually having an affair. When I first found out, I can remember feeling quite stunned despite the fact that I had plenty of time to get my head wrapped around the probability that he was, given that I was chasing the truth for quite some time. I was in shock and disbelief at his audacity and in no way did I expect to feel the depth of rage and betrayal that consumed me in the days, weeks and months that followed. I was experiencing extreme rage; it was rage directed at him and it was also rage directed inwardly towards myself for being his "patsy", I felt stupid, used and humiliated. In response to my rage, I resorted to writing about my feelings which was an excellent outlet helping to release some of the tension that my body was vibrating with. I had filled a multitude of foolscap note-pads with nonsensical writing expressing my erratic and volatile emotions. Whenever I decided to read back over what I had written, I found most of it to be illegible, a testimony to the potency of the emotion behind the words as they were penned. However, that really did not matter as it was a cathartic means for me to process everything I was experiencing and a release for the grief and rage I was feeling. The unexpected complexity of emotion was a revelation to me, why was this final betrayal so devastating to me, you would think that the infidelity would pale into significance compared to the verbal, physical, emotional, and psychological abuse I had already experienced from him. From the very beginning and over the duration of our relationship I had taken a physical, emotional and psychological battering. I was systematically denigrated by him in subtle and not so subtle ways which was compounded by my already existing fragile ego identity. I was held together by and depended on what I thought I had with him despite the abuse, I created a delusion or bought into his projected illusion that we were a strong and secure couple. I had invested my entire life into a relationship that in reality never existed. I tolerated neglect, continued and persistent abuse, abandonment, lack of emotional, physical and psychological support and forfeited my friends and family for a life with him. This is why I felt not only gutted by his betrayal but also devastated by how I had so easily betrayed myself, I was enraged and profoundly disappointed in both of us and I was consumed with grief over the demise of my non-existent illusory relationship.

The Awakening

"To ask the right question is already half the solution of a problem" – Carl Gustav Jung

It was during the months of enforced confinement while renovating our home that I experienced one of many profound life-changing "light bulb moments", probably due to the fact that I was voraciously reading books that had opened me up to engage in a broader and perhaps more lateral thinking. It occurred to me that I needed to ask myself two very important questions, firstly what does "love" mean to me? and secondly how do I need love to be expressed to me? I made the following list of qualities that quantified the expression of love for me, these included (without condition) honesty, respect, physical, emotional and psychological support and care, loyalty, fidelity and affection. These qualities reflected what I needed to feel loved by someone and they were also a reflection of how I give my love to others. I was immediately conscious of the fact that I was not receiving, nor did I ever receive any of these forms of love from my husband, this insight became the single most freeing moment of my life. I realised that I had taken responsibility for his shortcomings, compensating him by excusing, rationalising and minimising his behaviour. The weight of my feelings of shame, guilt, failure, and inadequacy regarding our relationship fell away, I felt relieved of a great burden. I was not aware until that moment that a part of me was clinging to some unconsciously driven desire to stay connected to this man and our abusive and dysfunctional relationship based on ingrained feelings of unreasoning loyalty. This "blind loyalty" as I came to understand much later, originated in my childhood a result of my own personal developmental dysfunction and was a significant component of my masochistic/burdened enduring character structure. This predominant character structure was also housing many limiting beliefs, along with an emotional and psychological naivete and a propensity for me to idealise reality.

With this awakening came the profound realisation that my husband was simply incapable of providing any of those qualities that defined love for me, they were not part of his fundamental character structure which was psychopathic/narcissistic. However, I do believe that he thought he truly loved me and he did to the best of his ability, albeit he could only love me with an inadequate understanding of how to care for and nurture another human-being. His behaviour was propelled by his narcissistic personality disorder and underpinned by his emotional, psychological and sexual immaturity. This made my decision to leave him easier and clearer, I needed to free myself from this relationship and I needed to find a way to do it that caused the least possible emotional and psychological harm to my children. The biggest hurdle was trying to manage my husband's violent temper, because he was determined that our relationship should remain as it is, even if it had to be for appearances only.

He alternated his threats, but essentially it narrowed down to two main threats, one was that the only way I would ever leave our home was in a box (as in coffin) and the other was that I could walk out the door any time I wanted but the children will remain with him. He knew my children were my world and that I would never under any circumstances leave them, using this threat as a manipulation to keep me tethered to him. I never thought to turn to anyone for help, I did not trust easily nor did I have confidence that any organisation could help my situation. I believed that I had to do this on my own and was also acutely aware that I might put whoever helped me in danger. Just to clarify, I was certainly cognizant that I could call the police and I'm sure they would have intervened on my behalf and perhaps I may have been able to procure a family violence intervention or restraining order. However, at that time I deemed that to be a temporary measure to take, knowing that the authorities could not hold him for long, this type of action by me would only enrage him and as soon as he was given the opportunity he would come after me with a vengeance.

I had first-hand knowledge of how spitefully he would respond to a restraining order, when I came across legal documents, he had hidden in the glove compartment of his car, information he kept concealed from me. I discovered these documents after I went searching for information to work out what had brought on a sudden random rageful attack aimed at me from him one morning while I was getting ready for work. I knew from experience that this outburst was slightly different and not the normal pattern of behaviour for him, immediately recognising that it must have been ignited by an external occurrence. Something or someone outside of our relationship had triggered what I believed to be a fear-based expression of rage. So, on an impulse, and while he was showering, I looked through his car to see if I could find a clue to what was going on. To my amazement, I found legal documents sequestered in the glove compartment, it appears that he had been arrested and was due to go to court this very morning for being in breach of an intervention order which had been placed on him by his ex-girlfriend. Apparently, she had broken up with him, he obviously did not take her rejection very well, he responded by going on a campaign of stalking, harassing and threatening her. This prompted her to place an intervention order against him which must have enraged him to the point where he decided to take action by breaking into her apartment while she was home and manhandling and menacing her.

Finding these documents answered a lot of questions as to the strange and erratic goings on that were occurring prior to the morning of this incident. I had noticed that over that last month or so my husband's unsound behaviour had escalated, he was smoking and drinking heavily, disappearing intermittently, at odd times and for varying periods of time. He would always come home decidedly angry and aggressive, looking for a reason to fight and for someone to take out his frustrations on, ultimately finding an easy target in me. I was to find out shortly that his perplexing behaviour was due to the fact that he was stalking his ex-girlfriend's home and her movements, combined with him being infuriated at her audacity to initiate an intervention order. He was outraged that he had lost his control over her and because she was getting on with her life. I found it to be profoundly ironic that he should get a taste of what it was like for me when I didn't know where or with whom he was spending his time and had to resort to stalking to find out. It was a divinely fateful turn-about for me to witness and for him to experience the same emotional distress, anxiety, frustration and anger that I had undergone not too long ago although for different reasons. His stalking was because he felt rejected and entitled, mine was because I needed to retrieve evidence of his lies and validate my feelings of distrust.

However, the bigger irony of the whole situation was that he was simultaneously being rejected by both women in his life, something his egotistic mind never expected, was ill prepared for or could accept. It must have stung, inflaming his already simmering anger into full blown rage, he was losing control of his life and it was rapidly spiralling down the sink hole. Not only was his intimate personal life in complete disarray, his business was suffering a loss because of his absences and some of his long-term male friendships were in jeopardy as a result of his neglect. When he finally accepted that he could not have her (she left the state) he decided to pour all his energy into sustaining our relationship, regardless of my opinion on the matter, deciding to use threats of violence and brute force when he felt it necessary. Our relationship from this point on resembled a battleground of strategies, I would take two steps forward and one step back while always trying to inch my way toward separation and freedom.

The Dance of War

Wars are not only fought on a battlefield, they are usually engineered from afar by a group of war strategists who are supposedly expert at defining objectives, administering procedures (tactical and logistical manoeuvres) and assessing risk factors. This is how I describe the drama and the series of events that took place during my bid for freedom, it was as if we were both engaging in combat tactics to achieve our personal goals. His aim was to coerce me into some type of arrangement that would keep me and the children with him. It was either to resume an intimate relationship with him as husband and wife or allow him to have a mistress but agree to maintain the façade of a happily married couple. My goal was to separate and start a new life without him in it and to achieve it with the least possible harm to our children, whose needs and wellbeing were my one and only absolute priority. He found it incredibly difficult to understand my desire to leave him, he thought that if he footed the bill for his family's life (his wife and children) regardless of whether he had an intimate relationship with his wife or not, that should be supremely satisfying for everyone involved. When I told him that I needed a peaceful life separate from him with just myself and my children. He replied with the statement that I could do that but I had to stay in the family home with him, he wanted things to go on as they did before, maintaining the "happily married couple" façade however with me condoning his extra marital affairs. He would continue to support our lifestyle economically and that I could do as I pleased (although this precluded me from having sex with another male) and he would do as he pleased as long as we stayed married and living in the house.

I never expressed to him all the reasons I had for wanting to leave him because I knew that he was incapable of understanding or accepting them. I desired above all else for my children and myself to live without fear of his temper, abuse, selfishness, and the constant melodrama that accompanied him. I craved a peaceful environment in which to raise my children and was entertaining the idea that eventually somewhere much further down the track to be able to enter into a mutually nourishing and rewarding relationship with someone special. He questioned me incessantly assuming that if I didn't want to accept his magnanimous offer that there must be another man in my life. I repeatedly denied this, however he did not believe me and had me followed by a private investigator for a couple of days, to determine if I was being truthful. I spotted the private detective one day while sweeping the front veranda of our home, but could not care less about his surveillance as I had nothing to hide and his report to my husband would only validate my integrity.

The fact that he had such a limited understanding of women and thought so little of them was highlighted to me time and time again, letting me know that he possessed a profound ignorance and an immaturity when it came to intimacy and human connection. Because I did not have some man waiting for me outside my marriage to take over responsibility for me, he could not comprehend me wanting to leave to be on my own. He completely dismissed the idea that I might have my own personal dreams, needs and desires assuming that they were either secondary or non-existent to what he prised most in the world money, possessions, financial holdings and social status. It was not possible for his misogynistic mind to comprehend why I would not accept either of his narcissistic, self-serving offers. He also expressed that if I did leave and were to enter into a relationship with another male with the intention of living together and/or marrying him that he would do everything in his power to prevent me from having access to my children. His ego dictated that there would never be another father figure in our children's life despite the fact that he was an absent and insufficient father himself.

This was the start of the most harrowing part of my life, I have tolerated many years of abuse from him up until this point. The abuse was to escalate to new heights as we entered into what can only be described as a psychological war by two embittered and beleaguered combatants' both desiring opposite outcomes. His campaign was to wear me down with a strategy that I was already familiar with, which was to start by being pleasant attempting to manipulate me into acquiescence, when this didn't work and it never did. It would very swiftly escalate into an expression of frustration with a verbal attack on me personally calling me names, telling me I was an inadequate wife and mother, followed by denigrating remarks about my hereditary origins and my family. As he spoke, he would gather momentum steadily increasing in aggravation and aggression, then he would invariably take an intimidating stance over me to make his point more effective. This would then be followed by an act of overt violence such as holding me down or against the wall by my throat, shoving and shaking me or throwing things at me.

This cycle of abuse continued on for the majority of nights for the next eighteen months, usually but not always after the children went to bed or after he arrived home from a late night out. There were days when he would call me from his car and start the process while he was driving around during the day, he would start by cajoling me and end with extreme verbal abuse. These were the same tactics he used in his face-to-face attacks and when I didn't tell him what he wanted to hear (which was that we would remain married) his anger would escalate into rage and then to threats of violence and he would always tell me not to leave the house because he was coming home. I could never ignore his phone calls, because if I did not answer them, he would call me incessantly until I did answer and be even more infuriated than usual. I would have to stay on the phone during his entire tirade (ranting and obscenities) until he hung up, there was nothing I could say that would placate him. Some days he would call me to abuse me, then hang up and call again and again repeatedly tormenting me, during these tirades he would frequently call me a whore.

First of all, "whore" was his preferred word to call me, he believed it belittled and denigrated me and when I was much younger it was indeed deeply hurtful, it would be impossible to put a figure on the number of times I had been called this over the entirety of our relationship. However, when I grew older and slightly wiser, I came to the conclusion that the actual word itself holds no insult for me and for two very good reasons. Firstly, I could not be a whore in the way he intended the word to imply because I was not arbitrarily sexually promiscuous or providing sexual services for money. Secondly, I realised it was a word among many invented and used by men to humiliate and castigate women. Their intention is to control and/or restrict her freedom to express her sexuality and to paint her in an offensive and distasteful light, implying she is a "bad girl" and therefore less than her female counterpart the "good girl." In the end it did not matter how many times he called me a whore it was not an insult, but that was my little secret. However, having said that, even though he had called me a whore enumerable times along with many other denigrating and debasing names and remarks, it was the potent hostility and forcefulness that accompanied his spiteful and malicious abusive remarks that often did have a harmful impact on me and over time took an emotional toll on me. To counteract some of the malevolence that was being hurled at me I employed a method wherein I would imagine an invisible shield around me with his words bouncing off it. It was my attempt to mitigate the impact of the vitriol that was being propelled at me and it helped on some occasions, but words carry energy and as hard as I tried not to let what he was saying hurt me, it did. It wasn't what he called me that affected me but more the hateful and vicious way in which he delivered it.

Fear

When you live with an abuser every day is a fight for survival, life is precarious for the one being abused, the cross a victim will bear is the burden of fear and uncertainty, not knowing if today will be their last day.

With each episode of abuse, he was becoming more insistent, earnestly trying his absolute utmost to wear me down and I was becoming more fatigued from the lack of sleep and the anxiety and fear that accompanied his threats of violence. He told me this could all stop (meaning his bullying and harassment), if I would agree to stay with him, I refused to give in, but rather entered into the psychological shuffle of "two steps forward one step back" with him. Whenever he went into one of his tirades, I would start off by saying that I was adamant that I wanted a separation, which he would not accept causing him to assert himself further. To try and deescalate proceedings, I would retreat slightly by providing him with a lesser concession, telling him that I would think about it, even though I had no intention of changing my mind. Every morning when he left home, I felt a modicum of relief, however as the day wore on the anxiety would build and as evening approached, I could feel myself slowly filling with dread. Nearly all of my awake time was consumed by feelings and thoughts that caused apprehension and distress, I was continually speculating about all the possible worst scenarios that might happen if he was to lose complete control of his senses.

The thing about fear is that it multiplies increasing in degree of intensity the longer it is allowed to germinate. It may start as a seed and given even the slightest molecule of nourishment will very quickly sprout, growing multiple shoots, becoming that weed that seems to flourish despite all efforts to eradicate it. When you live with an abuser there is an ever-present state of anxiety that exists, sometimes it is just a slight hum in the background of your mind and body that you can ignore, at other times it is a loud roar that commands your attention. The constant battle to manage my fear and anxiety was taking its' toll on me physically, emotionally, and psychologically. I was unable to focus, most of the time I operated on autopilot going through the motions that my life required. The physical repercussions that resulted from the presence of these pervasively stressful emotions that I was undergoing presented themselves in the form of various illnesses and an addiction to coffee and cigarettes. During this period of my life, I was experiencing cysts in my breasts, stomach ulcers, heartburn, headaches, migraines, pelvic pain, chronic neck, back and shoulder pain, sleeplessness and exhaustion. My family doctor treated me as best she could for the symptoms as they presented themselves but she could not treat me for the cause, that was something that needed psychological therapy.

Psychologically and emotionally, I was suffering constant distress, my general practitioner was not experienced at detecting psychological illness, which obviously is not her field of expertise, however, it was at the core of my illness issues. She was not aware that I was experiencing a condition known as PTSD (post-traumatic stress disorder), which would account for my feelings of being disorientated (forgetful and vague), dissociated (my mind and body felt disconnected) and my behaviour teetered between being manic at times (hyperarousal) or the opposite exhausted (hypo-arousal). Part of the exhaustion was due to fact that I was habitually "hypervigilant" for danger which did not allow for a restful or rejuvenating sleep, there was a part of my mind that would always be occupied with scanning for possible signs of threat. Sounds became amplified to my ears and so even the mildest noise could startle me, I found it difficult to be around large groups of people or places where the noise level was elevated as it was too disconcerting. I tried to keep up appearances to the outside world and to my children, I could not let anyone know what was happening so as not to incite their interest or enrage my husband.

I did not trust that anyone could help me and thought that they were likely to make it worse. This was extremely difficult at times as my closest and dearest girlfriends had noticed the changes in my physicality especially the rapid weight loss, persistent illnesses and in my personality with the loss of my attentiveness, positive nature, and sense of humour. I was very withdrawn and experiencing depression, I preferred to be alone and became quite reclusive, I was at the mercy of incessant "self to self" discussions (mind-chatter) which only worked to amplify already existing fearful thoughts (refer to self-talk book one). The negative self-talk was extremely detrimental to me because without new or external input I was playing the same record over and over again and had no ability to reality check the hysteric, compulsive and manic thoughts I was housing. Although not officially diagnosed at the time, I'm sure I was experiencing some level or type of mania. Along with all my symptoms, I also developed an intense distrust in all men, questioning their integrity, I thought they all harboured a dark side behind their friendly, artificial facades. I could not cope with anyone stepping into my intimate space apart from my children or my closest girlfriends and their children. If anyone else breached this space whether it was intentional (a kiss hello or goodbye or a hug) or it was accidental (someone coming up close next to or behind me in shop or restaurant) my body responded by going into hyper-arousal and my flight/fight/freeze response would kick in. This was the collateral damage from the years of abuse by my husband who would always intimidate and threaten me while standing in my personal space.

I was acutely aware of feeling deeply lonely and abandoned and was struggling with maintaining a connection to reality and the façade of normalcy. The dissociation caused by my constant state of terror was such that I often experienced being completely disconnected from my body as if I was outside myself, observing my life. I would find myself looking in the mirror at odd times during the day to see who was looking back at me. However, there was one remarkable happening that occurred on a routine basis that would without fail force me to connect back to my body, I refer of course to none other than my menstrual cycle. I welcomed if not relished the pain and discomfort that accompanied my monthly menses as it reminded me that I did indeed exist, compelling me to feel. How ironic that this natural phenomenon that throughout my youth I had often cursed as it interfered with fun times and some well laid plans with its' inopportune appearance, would become the one thing that brought me back to myself, when I most needed it.

Fear was my constant companion throughout my life with this man but never more so than the last eighteen months of our marriage, his steadily declining morality and sense of reality were reflected by his increasing short temper, irrationality and erratic behaviour. Fear robbed me of the ability to function fully in the present, it fogged the clarity and perception of the life I was living, causing my vision to literally become obscure. It inhibited me from openly expressing myself and it suppressed my freedom to speak authentically causing me to become a lesser version of myself. When I was consumed with fear my senses would automatically revert to their instinctive primordial function or "factory setting" if you will. They would scan for danger and prepare my "flight, fight or freeze" response which would lock me into survival mode and restrict my capacity to change the trajectory of this debilitating emotion. There were times when the fear was so magnified that it obliterated all thought, it felt as if I was hovering on the precipice between rationality and insanity. My fear was such that it became enthralling; it was slowly but surely becoming my habituated fall-back response that could very well have caused a complete psychological collapse and ultimately my defeat.

I knew intrinsically on a much deeper level that if I did not get a handle on my fear that I would spiral down the rabbit hole of terror knowing that I may lose the tenuous grip I still possessed on my mental stability. I was going to have to try to harness my fear if I was to gain any clarity and objectivity with my circumstances. Having a respectable amount of fear in a situation such as mine is paramount to keeping myself and my children safe, a healthy amount of fear keeps you sharp and helps to promote an acute awareness to possible danger, however, an overabundance of fear is crippling and obliterates all functional thought. For me, I realised that the key to overcoming this ordeal was to force myself to keep moving forward despite my fears, I needed to maintain my focus on the bigger picture, this was about my children's future, so I had no choice but to find a way through. Being proactive towards the future I desperately desired, reminded me of my purpose, it helped to restore reason and provided me with a measure of confidence to continue. Even though I could never fully banish my fear, I forced myself to manage it to the extent that enabled me to persevere with my original plan of action. Learning to contain my fear was by far one of the most difficult and challenging adversities I had to ever overcome.

Upon reflection, looking back from a place of safety, I asked myself the question, was the fear I was experiencing back then warranted, or was it amplified by my own irrational "self to self" talk. Could I have been wrong about how far my husband would really have gone if he had lost control and did what he threatened to do to me. I often contemplated whether I had at times worked myself in states of terror unnecessarily, perhaps in my mind I had exaggerated the circumstances anticipating the worst-case scenario and nothing less every time we altercated. Had incidental good fortune played a part or was he always capable of pulling himself back from the brink every time he lost his temper so as not to cause serious physical injury to me. State, national and international statistics reporting on the permanent maiming and deaths of female victims of abuse were telling me he would likely have not. It would only take a slight error in judgment on his behalf for me to become an addition to those statistics, my husband was six foot one and averaged between one hundred and ten, to one hundred and twenty kilos (seventeen to eighteen and half stone), I was five foot five and averaged between forty-six to fifty-four kilos (seven to eight and half stone) throughout our marriage. He had the advantage of his physical strength over me coupled with an uncontrollable temper and propensity to lash out without thinking. It would not take much to accidently or purposefully maim or kill me and I was very cognizant of that fact as was he. So, I concluded that even though there were occasions where I had worked myself up into highly charged terror filled states needlessly, I do truly believe that for the most part my profound experiences of fear were genuinely warranted. The fact remains that according to statistical reality, every argument with an abuser carries with it the potential for a violent, injurious, or lethal outcome.

Becoming the Wolf

The thing about narcissistic abusers is they believe themselves to be more intelligent than all other people who inhabit their world, particularly their victims. They think that because they have successfully lied to, controlled, manipulated and exploited their victim/s, that they have managed to outsmart them and are therefore superior in cleverness. This is a delusion they buy into because it feeds their ego-self, the truth is when a victim places their trust in someone they love and care for and if that trust is abused, it is not a sign of a lack of intelligence or discernment on their part. But more the sign of a human-being who has the capacity for real connectedness with another, they possess the ability to feel the positive emotions necessary for a rewarding relationship based on mutual trust, care and love. When a victim's trust is abused, it usually comes as shock to them, they are blindsided because they have placed their faith in someone whom they expect to reciprocate those same feelings. This is not an indication that a victim lacks foresight or intellect but rather a natural expectation that the one they love and care for will return it in equal measure. The biggest mistake an abuser makes is revelling in their feelings of "supposed superiority", thinking they are smarter than their victim and it usually heralds their downfall at some point in their life.

When a victim awakens to the reality that they are undeniably being abused than this is the opportunity to acknowledge the facts and accept the truth as painful as that is. A victim cannot label themselves as being stupid or a fool, nor can others accuse or label them either, as it perfectly natural to want to love and be loved by their chosen someone. Most of us seek to enter into a committed relationship with optimism, anticipation and positive expectation, hoping that the relationship will blossom into something mutually rewarding for both. When this relationship becomes an abusive one it is certainly not because of ignorance on behalf of a victim, it is simply that a predator has taken advantage of the trust that has been placed in them. However, underestimating the intelligence and cunning of a victim or believing a victim is sufficiently cowed and therefore rendered passive and powerless is the abusers "Achilles Heel". This is why it is possible to turn the tables on the abuser wherein they become the ones who are blindsided and shocked by the actions taken by their victim.

I came to this understanding through my quest for knowledge and after much personal self-reflection. I made the personal determination that even though my husband had an advantage over me with his physical strength, he was not psychologically or emotionally stronger than me. One of his major disadvantages was that he was psychologically and emotionally immature, which often caused him to be at the mercy of his volatile emotions and not in control of them. The drawback of being controlled by his emotional states of being is that most of his decisions are made without much thought. His narcissism was such that it closed him off to learning anything new, he believed he knew all he needed to know in life and was not interested in educating himself further. As for myself I had realised that despite my fears, I was actually more robust than him, and emotionally and psychologically more rational, which was to become a valuable resource that I would call on time and time again. I had learned that a person who has completely surrendered to a particular emotional state, regardless whether it is a positive or negative emotion, then they are unable to think clearly. They will be in an "all-feeling" mode, which essentially means that they have de-linked from the ability to think rationally as their mind and body is completely absorbed by a particular emotion. Knowing this gave me a deeper insight into the understanding of both our behavioural interactions and responses and how to better manage them.

As I was going through this traumatic period with my husband, I was also simultaneously trying to gain as much knowledge, assistance and guidance as I could. I went to seminars and entered into therapy with a psychologist, I was trying to deal with the aftermath of his affair and at the same time trying to find a way to understand him, myself and our relationship. The more I learned the more enlightened I became, realising that there was a great depth and an emotional and psychological complexity to our individual and relationship dysfunction. I was reading numerous publications (books, magazines, periodicals and articles) containing mixed subject matter that included genres such as, self-help, personal development, relationship dysfunction, spiritual ideology, psychology and philosophy. Each publication that I read at the minimum, gave me something to think about and at the most provided me with varying degrees of insight, orientation (helped me get my bearings), cognizance, and growth. However, I could not find a clear path or solution to escape my present volatile situation in a way that would ensure permanent freedom without retaliation from a psychopathic disgruntled ex-partner. At that time, I was not confident in seeking policing and court intervention or refuge in a shelter thinking that their protection would only be temporary and that I would forever be worried about being stalked, harassed and be incessantly fearful of vengeful retaliation from my angry and retributive husband.

During the process of arming myself with knowledge, I could not help but take an inevitable psychological and emotional journey inward, which helped to create new pathways of understanding by expanding my perception of myself, others, and the world at large. This new found wisdom and experience aided in laying down the foundations for real growth to transpire, acting as a catalyst to affect the initial significant positive changes within myself. However, it was later when I entered into my course to become a Soul Centred Psychotherapist that I realised that I was barely scratching the surface of what I really needed to know and understand about myself. I had been introduced into the world of psychotherapy through a girlfriend who was participating in a course to become a psychotherapist herself. She was not aware of my personal circumstances at that time but we shared a mutual interest in mind/body therapies and I was completely fascinated with the subject matter she was learning. It was not long before I enrolled in the same psychotherapy course albeit a year behind her. It was through my study of character structure and defence theory that led me to come to a life changing and vital determination.

I theorised that in order to understand and deal with the psyche of my abusive perpetrator "The Wolf," that I had to comprehend the world through his eyes. If I could see the world through his eyes, I might be able to better anticipate his thought processes and thereby increase the probability of out-strategizing him. In other words, I had to "become the wolf to escape the wolf" and so I poured all my energy into investigating both our behavioural patterns, our defences and what drove them. I formed a flexible plan of action aimed at overcoming the most apparent obstacles, my intention was to hopefully outmanoeuvre him. My objectives included the following, circumventing any possible violent consequences, reframing our verbal discourse to seed new thoughts, manipulate his recalcitrant extended family and friends to my way of thinking, who were hindering any progress I made, and lastly preparing my children psychologically and emotionally for the separation. I had to make it easier for him to leave and I had to create a reason for him to want to leave, perhaps providing him with some kind of incentive if that were even possible. I was in no way confident or feeling the least bit assured of any success, this was a learn as you go deal that required immense fortitude and a great deal of luck.

By becoming the wolf, I began to understand his needs, desires and ambitions, along with his personal, social and professional concerns and fears, I was better equipped to anticipate what he might be thinking and how he might respond to any given situation. I learned that several essential issues had to be addressed in order to breach his defence system to clear the path for his psyche to accept a new and different outlook towards our situation. I had to steer him in the direction I wanted him to take through the subtle seeding of ideas and they had to be persistent and consistent in content in order for the possible new thought to take root in his consciousness. I started by steering our arguments away from the topic of whether I was staying with him or leaving him by suggesting that he needed his freedom. I grasped onto and used the narrative of empathising with how he had never really had the opportunity to pursue and enjoy his youth as he married too young and that the single life was the life that best suited him and that there was nothing wrong with that.

His preoccupation with his image was a major obstacle that I had to overcome, he was driven by the acute need to maintain the façade of "successful business man and loving father/husband" (a consequence of his narcissistic disorder). My aim was to convince him that it was okay for him to move out and live the single life that he desires, needs to, and should be living and that he can do this without the shame of failure and guilt of disappointing friends and family. I had to address this impediment to my end game on two levels simultaneously, the first was directed at my husband (a plan already in action) and the second was directed towards his closest and most influential friends and family members. Regrettably, it was his close male confidants and family members that were contradicting my efforts to move him on, they were opposing any thoughts he might have entertained of moving out. This is likely to due to the fact that they were reared with the same misogynistic ideology as my husband, believing that divorce is a sign of failure on a husband's behalf and not an acceptable alternative in their family (religiously and culturally motivated).

They mistakenly thought that the choice to stay married was his alone, presuming he held the seat of power to keep us together and that they were doing my children and I a favour by vetoing any ideas he might have had to leave. To address this issue, I had to rely on and use the weight of my own personal relationship with these individuals to change their stance and bring them into alignment with my objective. In order to do this, I had to meet with those closest to him individually (divide and conquer) by surreptitiously creating opportune circumstances to be alone with each of the significant parties involved. I had to convince these individuals that my husband needed to move on and live the single life that he deserved and should be living and how I fully support him moving on. I also had to convince them that the separation will not be harmful to my children, in fact I managed to persuade them into believing the opposite, that we would thrive.

Even though the subterfuge I felt I had to employ with certain friends and family went against my ethical grain, I believed it to be a necessary evil when I was fighting for both mine and my children's survival. I was morally conflicted at that time as I was possessed of a fervent contempt for lies and the direct and collateral damage it reaps for all who are involved. It might even seem hypocritical to some of you that I had to employ disingenuity to achieve my goals, however I considered this a necessary and justifiable tool to be used in the war I had grudgingly been forced into by husband's misconduct and immorality. I am in no way defending my actions but rather further explaining that there is a certain level of stress and anxiety that accompanies every decision made and action taken that compounds the already existing fear and apprehension that I was undergoing. There was nothing easy about any of this, each day I would start with the same intention which is to fight back, hold my ground, and if I'm lucky make some progress. However, it was physically, emotionally and psychologically exhausting, the two steps forward, one step back tactic appeared to keep us both at an impasse, it became a battle of wills and there seemed no end in sight.

Remember I was bedding down at night on a narrow leather couch in our loungeroom, which was extremely uncomfortable and contributed to the difficulty of finding a level of relaxation that was conducive for a restful night's sleep. Not getting enough sleep amplified my fragile emotional state heightening my fears and anxieties, making it difficult for me to sustain an objective state of being. We were approximately twelve to fourteen months into this battle, I had experienced a particularly harrowing day in which he had called me numerous times throughout the day with a diatribe of verbal harassment followed by an onslaught of personal insults and threats of violence. This left me feeling exhausted, disillusioned, depressed and desperate, so much so that I was contemplating giving in to my husband's demands. I went to bed (the couch) that night with my emotions in turmoil tossing and turning and then finally drifting off into a fitful slumber.

The next morning in early hours of dawn I was woken up with a feeling of being entirely swathed in a beautiful soft warm blanket of light. The warmth surrounded me and was moving through me, penetrating my heart heating me from the inside out. It felt like I was being given an infusion of what can only be described as love, a feeling of euphoria spread over me. I opened my eyes to discover that I was not alone there was an elderly woman sitting in a chair just to the right of me, she was asleep, looking like she had nodded off while watching over me. The feeling of warmth that I was experiencing felt as if it was coming directly from her but enveloping us both in a field of loving energy. I can remember asking myself if I was dreaming, was this some type of illusion conjured up by my lack of sleep, but at the same time I knew in my heart of hearts it was not. I was not a person who was given to flights of fancy, nor did I possess a belief in any particular singular religious or spiritual doctrine, however this was the most beautiful, enigmatic phenomenon to ever happen to me.

The woman looked familiar to me as she was garbed in the distinct clothing that the women of my father's village in the former Yugoslavia had worn when I had visited back in 1970. It occurred to me that this looked like my uncles widowed wife "baba Anca", the woman who had nursed me when I had dislocated my ankle on my visit to that village when I was just eight years old, this could be my uncle's widowed wife. She was dressed all in black and her head was wrapped in a black scarf with just her face visible, she was radiating love and it was directed at me and at the same time she was communicating to me without opening her eyes or uttering a sound. Her message to me was that I was not alone and that she was and will always remain with me, protecting and watching over me. I never wanted the connection to end but it did, however I was left with the knowledge that I was never ever walking this earth alone, that there was a much bigger picture than the reality I was living, something perhaps beyond my comprehension but nevertheless I was not to despair. This experience gave me the strength to keep fighting and wiped away the feelings of residual fear, loneliness and abandonment that always lingered after my husband's abusive episodes and it helped to sustain me through many unpleasant and daunting experiences that were to follow.

As we were nearing the end of what would have been the eighteenth month of our siege, I could not endure any more of the abuse and was too physically, emotionally, and psychologically fatigued to continue the battle. I decided that I had had enough and surrendered myself and the situation to the powers that be, letting go of what was to transpire as a result. With this decision I felt both deeply disillusioned and at the same time contrarily relieved having relinquished the constant exhausting apprehension, tension and concentrated attention that was needed to sustain me for each battle. I decided I would tell him of my decision (which contained conditions) this very night and deal with whatever the outcome would be, however I was certainly not prepared for the shock of what was to happen next.

As it turned out he came home that same night just as my children and I were finishing our evening meal and he was in an aggressive, agitated state of arousal, he marched up to the kitchen table and addressed the children stating "your mother and I are getting a divorce, your mother hates me." My children and I were shocked to say the least and sat in stunned silence, we were not sure how to respond because he was so hostile and he looked menacing. We gave him a blank stare; however, we were all secretly relieved that he was going to leave and I was personally distinctly elated that he had surrendered just before I was to concede to his demands. He continued on to malign my character to the children making me the villain in the scenario, which didn't bother me personally at all, however it was not okay with me that he was hurting the children by doing this. A few days later he found a two-bedroom apartment, he was to move out in a couple of weeks. I was happy to expedite matters by packing everything for him while he was at work, including kitchen utensils, dinner-ware, and bedding. He furnished his new residence and placed two single beds in his spare room for our children for the "supposed" shared visits we had agreed to.

It did not occur to me at the time, however later and upon reflection, I realised that the game plan I had devised to convince him to move on of his own volition had in fact worked for me in the end. This outcome came about due to the combination of the strategies that I employed and was a culmination of four key factors working together. By firmly holding to my purpose or end game if you like, had helped to sustain me through my darkest hours. I had to continually remind myself of the much larger picture and that the freedom and peace I was seeking for myself and my children hung in the balance. I had to remain committed to the tactical plan I had formed despite the frustration, disillusionment, and backsliding that the "two steps forward, one step back" process had caused. I had to face, endure, and surmount the prevailing feelings of fear, anxiety, and uncertainty that remained omnipresent throughout the entire ordeal and lastly, I believe it was also due to my reticent but pugnacious fighting spirit coupled with my inherently determined nature that got me over the line.

He chose to believe that he had been forced to leave, and that the dissolution of our marriage was due to my stubborn pride and unwillingness to forgive, thereby shifting the focus off his bad behaviour and placing the blame on me, this was the narrative that he espoused to friends and family. I expected nothing less from him, his narcissism was such that it would only allow him to default into playing one of two roles either that of the "hero" or the "victim," he needed to play the victim, while simultaneously minimising his abusive actions. The truth is that he was leaving because I had created favourable circumstances in which he could leave, he was able to "save face" (his dignity) with his family and friends, without disgracing himself or tarnishing his reputation. It did not bother me that he needed to place the blame on me and thereby lessen his culpability for the demise of our marriage. Simply because we both knew the truth, it was not important what others thought of me when taking into consideration what was being gained for myself and my children, the most important fact was that he was moving out, this was a prodigious blessing. He was however right about me personally, yes it was true; I was indeed no longer willing to forgive him his abusive actions, and yes, I was stubborn, this is of course if you refer to what I believe to be tenacity as obstinacy.

The uncanny or coincidental irony of it all of course is that he finally conceded defeat on the same day that I had made the decision to surrender to his demands. This caused me to speculate about the "bigger picture" and the possibility that there exists a subtle kind of metaphysical, karmic, or cryptic universal law at play, where there is a delicate balancing act between taking the necessary steps to make things happen in your life and knowing when to let go of the desired outcome. However, regardless of whether the events that took place that same night following my decision to submit to his demands were fateful or not, I was most profoundly taken aback that something unexpected but providential had occurred in my life. It is these types of synchronistic events that surprise and baffle me simultaneously, I am, as always, mystified by the universes complex but capricious forces and by its' wonderfully serendipitous nature.

Shattered Illusions

"There is no coming to consciousness without pain" – Carl Gustave Jung

Part of our agreement to part ways was that we would continue to renovate the family home that I was currently living in with the children, with the intention for it to be sold as part of the divorce settlement. This home was a hundred-year-old, solid brick, Edwardian, that I fell in love with the moment I stepped foot into its foyer five years earlier. My husband was a builder and so he spear-headed the coming renovation, however it was to take another year to complete, during which time we had to frequently unpleasantly interact. During the renovation the entire property was overrun with tradesmen who started work at seven am every morning, there was very little privacy and the ever-present clamour of building noise. The only part of my home that I could seek solace in during the day was my bedroom, although it wasn't long before it grew to feel oppressive. As I looked out my bedroom window the view was completely disrupted by the scaffolding that the tradesmen had erected, it blocked the direct sunlight causing it to appear fractured, making me feel like I was in a prison of sorts and it was a constant unpleasant reminder of the chaos that was going on all around me.

I often wondered whether the scaffolding and the changes being made to upgrade our home were an external manifestation of my internal feeling of being trapped and the transformations that were simultaneously taking place within me. The point is I actually was evolving psychologically, albeit grudgingly and it was a slow but certain process, which was happening to me whether I wanted it to or not, propelled along by some intangible external force of nature. When I say "external force" I am referring to the natural evolutionary processes of life that we cannot slow down or stop because they are a result of decisions made and actions taken. It did not help that I was a procrastinator when it came to making decisions, incessantly weighing up the pros and cons, afraid of making the wrong choice and having my children bear the consequences. I also personally did not deal well with change (a consequence of my childhood upbringing) and was therefore quite cautious if not resistant to even the smallest modification to my life. Unfortunately, my life situation was forcing me to make internal and external transformations, demanding that I relinquish control of how, when and where those changes were to occur.

You would think the hard part was over when my husband moved out and my children and I were free to start our lives without the constant feeling of oppression from our abuser, but I'm sorry to say it was not, it marked the end of the first part of our journey and the beginning of our next. The elation I felt of being free was very quickly to be overshadowed by the fallout from being the victim of long-term abuse, it was yet another naive self-deception (illusion) that I had to address and overcome. It soon became apparent that I had an even more difficult personal trek to undertake in my journey towards physical, emotional and psychological wellness and wholeness. The truth was I felt deeply fractured by past events and kept imagining myself in the image of a puzzle with the pieces all there but disconnected. I did not feel whole, I did not know who I was, which was distinctly alarming for me because in my marriage I had a clear and definite idea of who I was. I defined myself as a devoted mother and wife, adept at managing domestic, social and work commitments, I was staunchly loyal to those I loved and I was the person who could be relied upon when times were tough. It was a persona I fostered with relish, which was glued together by my unrelenting standards, driven by my chronic aspiration towards perfectionism and underpinned by my desperate need for acceptance, praise, affection and love.

This ego-ideal I held of myself had become another statistic to add to the growing list of shattered illusions, because it was secured together by the principles that I had formed and needed to project to compensate for my unconsciously motivated deep-seeded feelings of un-deservingness, unworthiness and failure. Without the safety net of my ego-ideal I became completely bereft, like a boat adrift at sea without a rudder, I felt thoroughly disenfranchised, vulnerable and depressed. I was spiralling downward into a dark and unknown abyss, feeling alone, insignificant and abandoned, I had no self-esteem and had lost trust in others and the world at large. I was also suffering from symptoms of PTSD (post-traumatic stress disorder) although I was not aware of it at the time, my symptoms included sleeplessness, dissociation, an inability to concentrate, fatigue, chronic headaches, neck, back and shoulder pain, stomach ulcers, a hypersensitivity to loud and unexpected sounds and I was in a constant state of anxiety.

Perhaps I was feeling so much all at once because the imminent threat of violence was removed from our home and my mind and body was now permitted to experience the effects of the intense traumas that I had undergone but was never allowed to feel. The only thing that kept me clinging to reality was my love for my children and my need to be there for them, I was resolute that they not be further harmed by my husband's issues or my own issues of unhappiness and disillusionment. My family doctor did try to help me by treating some of the medical issues such as the stomach and indigestion ailments with medication, the sleeplessness with sleeping pills and the depression with anti-depressants. However, after trying half a sleeping pill and finding myself too disorientated to drive the kids to school the next morning, I threw them out. As for the anti-depressants I was unable to bring myself to fulfil the script, firstly, I could not countenance not having complete control over my faculties secondly, I did not want my hypervigilance impaired in any way and thirdly because I felt it was vitally important that I be able to feel every emotion whether it was good or bad.

However, there were many times when I wished I didn't feel the need to be so vigilant and controlled and envied those who could find solace or numbness at the bottom of a bottle or through the use of licit or illicit drugs. I can remember needing and wanting to sleep all the time and did so at every opportunity that presented itself in an effort to escape the persistent and undesirable thoughts and emotions that tormented me. I was riddled with guilt over my bad choice of life-partner which had resulted in a relationship that had not provided my children with the healthiest and most nourishing environment that they like all children deserved, and I was also feeling extreme shame at having failed them as a mother. For a while I teetered between wallowing in self-pity and self-hate, I was filled with rage against my husband and rage against some of his family and friends, I could not come to terms with the fact that no one could see what he was doing to us or tried to stop him when they did. These volatile emotions were exacerbating my already existing physical illnesses to the point where I was becoming extremely unwell. I thought that there was something innately flawed in me and that for reasons beyond my comprehension I was deemed undeserving of better or being punished for the poor choices I had made and now had to pay for.

These thought patterns had to stop and they eventually did, I had hit what I considered at the time to be my lowest point and realised that if I continued down this path that I could not possibly even try to be a good mother to my children.

They deserved the best life possible even though I myself felt that I didn't, I had to change my direction, pull myself together and concentrate all my efforts on my children's wellbeing and happiness and overcoming the challenges that lay ahead. I shifted my focus from my personal issues and discovered that there was indeed a bottom to my supposed bottomless pit of self-pity and self-flagellation and now that I reached it, there was only way to go and that was back up towards the light.

I had to come to terms with the fact that my relationship with my husband was a projected illusion and that my persona (ego-self) which I had cultivated throughout my life was also a projected illusion. It was a construct of parts designed to fulfil others' expectations and needs in order to receive approval. It was a way in which I could procure the much-desired affection, acceptance and love I needed from everyone who had been pivotal in my life at one time or another, my parents, teachers, friends, work associates, employers and my husband. Coming to terms with the realisation that this "identity" I created had been stripped away from me laying me bare was immensely disorientating and distressing, I felt lost without her. Facing the truth about myself was painful and deeply unnerving, I did not know who I was and I did not know who I wanted to be, all my authentic likes, dislikes, dreams, and aspirations that I had once entertained as a burgeoning young woman were curtailed when I entered a relationship with my abuser. It was difficult to even remember what they were as they were never given time to manifest or the opportunity to grow and flourish.

It's Not Over

After we sold our property, we settled on a division of assets that favoured him, this was one of the prices I had to pay to attain my and my children's freedom. Money is important there is no denying it however I wanted out and I wanted out safely, so I agreed to whatever financial terms he put before me, knowing that I could have received a hell of a lot more. I knew that money and the feelings of power and success it brought my husband meant absolutely everything to him and parting with it would bring feelings of rage and revenge had I attempted to take more than he was willing to give. His narcissistic personality disorder required that he project the persona of a successful businessman and portray the image of a wealthy playboy, therefore he needed the lion's share of our collective assets to do so. I also did not want to endanger my children in any way, knowing from firsthand experience that he would retaliate if he felt threatened in any way, he had never directly threatened or physically harmed the children, however I did not want anything to happen to me and for the children to be put into his fulltime care. This did not mean that the children were not harmed emotionally and psychologically through witnessing the abuse that was occurring in our relationship. I made their safety and well-being my priority so as to avoid or at least minimise the children participating in or bearing witnessing to further drama and conflict, particularly that associated with separation and divorce, trying my absolute best to ensure it went as smoothly as was possible.

I did not breathe a word of my abuse or my husband's abusive predilections to anyone bar my closest girlfriend and my therapist whom I trusted with my and my children's lives. This was always part of my "big plan" it was a strategy which played a large part in allowing me the opportunity to separate with a lower risk of retaliation from my husband. It was to my benefit to maintain my silence about the abuse at that time and I did so, there were many close friends and some family who speculated that we separated because he had an affair. I did not care what other people thought or talked about and never spoke to anyone about my real reasons for leaving. I did not in any way wish for gossip to reach the ears of my young children, I never corroborated or denied any gossip knowing we would soon become yesterday's news and we did. I made a decision very early on that there are several things I must never do which I have witnessed in other relationships between acrimonious divorced couples that is extremely harmful to children. Even though there were times when I struggled not to, I never engaged in verbally maligning or denigrating my husband's character in front of my children (I vented privately) while they were growing up, and I never used my children as an instrument for vengeance or as a bargaining chip, or tool to manipulate him or a situation.

It eventually became impossible to complete the renovations and live in our family home, so I moved into a rental home with my children, during this time my husband had settled into his apartment and into single life. However, despite having the freedom to do as he pleased, he was also just as determined to persist in managing me and the children and to continue to assert himself in our lives unnecessarily. He was regularly turning up unannounced to my home and incessantly asking my children personal questions about me, he wanted to know where I went, who I spent time with, who visited my home etc. When he came to pick up the children for a visitation, I would try to speak to him at the door, but he would always attempt to gain entry on the pretext that he either wanted a glass of water or needed to use the bathroom. To avoid conflict in front of my children I would allow him entry, leave him with my children and then remove myself to another part of the house. This was one of his manipulative bullying tactics, he wanted to assert that he was still in charge, a show of power to let me know that he felt he still had the right to intrude upon my life anytime he pleased.

I abhorred his presence and could not wait for him to leave; I was forced to tolerate his intrusions to keep the peace and I did so under great duress. Our children only stayed with him one night a week and accompanied him to family functions or lunch on a Sunday at the grandparents, this was by mutual agreement between the two of us which I had orchestrated so that they had the least possible exposure to his volatile personality. He did not know it at the time but my children disliked staying at his apartment with him, particularly if he was in a bad mood as he would divide his time between watching football and maligning my character. This one night a week dwindled down within about six months to no overnight visits from my children, they still however accompanied him to family events. This suited him as he had fully engaged himself into single life and was enjoying his freedom, happy to leave the full-time care of his children to me. His victimisation of me never ceased, he continued to verbally harass and threaten me by phone and in person whenever he was so inclined adhering to an old pattern that whenever something went going wrong in his life, he would take it out on me.

He would call to berate me about the smallest things, criticising every aspect of the way I parented our children, he deemed my parenting skills inadequate. These calls could be repeated throughout a single day and continue for days until he felt he had sufficiently vented his frustrations out on me. This became a pattern of behaviour which would increase in intensity when he was not involved in a relationship with another female and decrease when he was. However regardless of the circumstances whenever he worked himself up into a fury, he would drive to my home to berate and threaten me in person. This kept my nervous system on high alert, keeping me continually hypervigilant for danger, it was impossible to ever truly relax even though we lived in different locations. We were still at risk with the potential for possible harm still hanging over our heads, this would often fuel my imagination and send my defensive vigilance into overdrive making me as anxious and as fearful as I was when I lived with him.

The rental home that the children and I moved into during the last part of the renovations on the main house was in a street by the name of "Hartington." Every room was painted with a medley of colours as if the painter could not decide on a colour scheme, it was kind of quirky but also welcoming in a unique and charming way. The walls and the ceiling of the master bedroom were painted a muted olive green and the ceiling roses and cornices which were intricate in design, were hand painted with various soft shades of rose. I was hoping to find some peace while living in this new environment, to catch my breath so to speak so that I could regain my equilibrium and think about how to approach the future. This peace was frequently interrupted by my husband who was disregarding my personal boundaries and invading my privacy creating pervasive feelings of tension and trepidation which were at times proving difficult to manage. There were occasions when I thought I heard his voice or the sound of him clearing his throat, a distinct noise he used to make, even though he was not actually there, however it would set my mind and body into high alert until I realised that it was only my imagination.

Sometimes I would wake up in fright from a nightmare that was the re-enactment of past traumatic events and sometimes I would just wake up thinking I heard him calling my name. I later came to understand that these were some of the symptoms of PTSD (post-traumatic stress disorder) that I was experiencing. During my stay in this home, my time was divided between home duties, my children and studying to be a psychotherapist, I had to do my assignments after the children went to bed usually until the early hours of the morning. Studying proved to be an excellent distraction from my personal issues and a great blessing because the more I learned about human behaviour the more I understood about my past dysfunctional dynamic with my ex-husband.

I learned in great detail about our character structures, the underlying beliefs which drove those structures and the defences that were created as a result. This transitional home inspired healing, it was a safe haven or sorts providing me with my first real glimpse of what it would feel like to be free from constant turmoil, anxiety and fear. Approximately eight months later the children and I bought a home close to their respective schools and their friends, I did not want their life to change any more than it already had. This was to be our home for the next six years in which abusive encounters with my ex-husband were to continue for whatever reason he deemed important enough and at any given time. He would randomly turn up unannounced and uninvited to verbally harass and threaten me in person or he would phone me. However, there was one distinct incident that occurred that is highlighted in my memory. In this particular instance, he started out with his usual MO (mode of operation), he phoned me with a bone to pick. I could tell he was looking to start an argument, which he did no matter how hard I tried not to and as usual this led to him very quickly losing control of his temper. He ordered me to wait for him, he was coming to see me in person (he was not far away). My daughter was home at the time and I can remember distinctly thinking I am not going to allow him to catch us at home and defenceless. I grabbed my car-keys, telling my daughter that her dad was coming to our home, he was in a temper, and that we needed to get out of the house immediately.

We both jumped into the car, I reversed out of the drive and took off just as he was coming around the corner, he saw us and gave chase, I turned right he followed me and over-took my car, cutting us off on the diagonal leaving me no-where to go so I jumped on the breaks bringing the car to an abrupt stop. He wound down his passenger side window and indicated that I should do the same which I did, he proceeded to abuse me verbally, however his tirade suddenly stopped when the owner of the home we were in front of came out to use his garage. He looked at us taking in the situation and frowned which caused my husband to reverse his car and take off with a promise that this was not over. One small but significant consolation came from this incident for me which was that I felt that I had grown in courage, I realised later that I had acted in a positive way for the first time by removing myself and my daughter from a potentially dangerous situation. The usual response to my ex-husbands tirades and threats of violence were to stay put, thinking that if I was to leave my home, he would only come back later and be much angrier than he already was, risking greater violence. My body would automatically go into the "freeze" response and fear would take hold giving reign to my imagination causing me to panic.

In this incident instead of freezing I took flight which had helped me in two ways firstly, running when in danger is a more advantageous survival response than inertia and secondly, I was able to lead him away from our home. My home was supposed to be my sanctuary not my prison, I wanted to protect the integrity of this new space to establish an environment free of the stain of abuse. Calling the police was not an option for me at that time because even though I knew they could save the day, I had to think about tomorrow and the day after that, how long could law-enforcement and the judicial system hold him at bay. In the past he had broken the restriction of a restraining order issued against him by an ex-girlfriend and assaulted her, what was to stop him from coming after me. Perpetrators of abuse are well aware that the threat of violence works just as effectively as the act of violence itself, it is mutual in nature, the aim is to manipulate, control and/or punish a victim. Violence or the threat of violence can also have an enduring effect on a victim that does not end when the threat is removed, even if the removal of the threat is permanent. A victim of abuse whether it is a singular traumatic event or on-ging trauma such as mine, will inevitably carry the memories of these events bearing the physical, emotional and psychological scars as a result. I had been in an abusive relationship from the age of eighteen years until just over fifty years of age, it had been approximately thirty-two years of abuse.

The abusive harassment reduced moderately as my children entered their late teens, early twenties as they were gaining in independence and growing in maturity, and so he had little reason to contact me regarding their activities. However, the abusive occurrences became considerably minimal when he entered into an exclusive relationship with a young woman he met on a holiday.

This was his first committed relationship since our divorce, it seems that they became enamoured with each other quite quickly and so it wasn't long before she moved into his apartment with him. She became his focus, absorbing all his energy into sustaining his new relationship, she was approximately twenty years his junior so I am pretty certain there would have been some teething problems to overcome. Unfortunately, I could not help but think that he likely found a new outlet for his unresolved volatile emotions and felt a deep regret that this new love interest could quite likely become the target of his abusive behaviour. I quietly hoped that I was wrong about my assumptions for her sake, and from what I had subsequently learned from my children it appeared that he had mellowed somewhat and was showing a different more settled side of himself. Having said that I cannot lie, I did selfishly feel relief whenever he shifted his focus off me and the children.

However, even though he had stopped constantly harassing me, I never relaxed my vigilance, it was never going to be a simple process to shut off my innate defensive behaviours. These were the thoughts and feelings that had become my habituated protective instinctual responses that were essential elements for most of my adult life. The fact that he interacted with my children meant that I still had a link to him, even though over time our communication had dwindled down to a rare occasion. Slowly but surely, I was able to relax my guard and for the most part managed to attain the privacy, peace and solace I was seeking and needed for myself and my children. It took a good ten years to get to this point, although I remained cautiously vigilant over his interactions with my children.

Regrettably, he did not evolve emotionally or psychologically during the subsequent ten years post our separation, nor did his committed relationship change him in any way and so he invariably found himself embroiled in some drama or another in his life whether it was personal or professional. Throughout the intervening years there were significant occasions when he stepped up in his role as a father to help his children financially, paying for private school fees, first cars and other specific instances when they needed a cash injection, for which the children were extremely thankful. However, his fundamental narcissistically driven character traits and beliefs remained the same, and so it was inevitable that he would clash with my children as they grew in independence and individuality. This was to be the cause of some conflict in the continuity of his relationship with them and was a sustained source of disappointment to them.

During those first ten years of separation, I had completed my course to become a Soul Centred Psychotherapist starting a private practice in a backyard studio in the new home that was purchased in the divorce settlement. My priority was the children's well-being and my life was dedicated to that cause, I wanted them to have the best life possible and I knew that I needed to keep working on myself and my issues for both our benefit. I also chose not to pursue a personal relationship for myself, I wasn't emotionally prepared for or psychologically healthy enough to engage in an intimate connection with another male, nor did I want another man in my children's lives until they became independent young adults. However, there were many times I profoundly felt the absence of having a partner who I could have shared my concerns with and who could have helped lighten the load with the child rearing. The feelings of natural parental stress and anxious worry were especially compelling through those teenage years when I was traversing all the issues that were associated with the children when growing from adolescence into adulthood.

As the children grew older and were gaining in autonomy, there were distinct moments when I felt a poignant loneliness, missing the shared intimacy that can only be experienced with a loving partner. I never had the courage to change my personal circumstances throughout those intervening years as I was struggling with residual feelings of inadequacy and low self-esteem while trying to re-build my confidence, dignity and sense of worth. I was also troubled by my ex-husbands constant shadowing presence in my life and couldn't bring myself to burden or expose a new partner with this dilemma. There seemed to be this pervasive feeling that my husband was a temperamental and unpredictable danger, who would forever be a persistent source of apprehension for me and the children, whether his presence in our lives was tangible or not. Now that we lived in separate premises and different suburbs, I became painfully aware that the children and I were somewhat at a disadvantage not knowing where he was at any given time or when he was going to appear on our doorstep. When we were living with him, I pretty much knew when he was coming home giving me time to prepare myself and my children for his return, in gaining our freedom from living with his ever-present harmful and volatile presence, we were paradoxically still beset with those same persistent feelings of apprehension now that we were not. The not knowing was as detrimental and disconcerting to our well-being and sense of equanimity as the knowing, there was still a price to be paid for our freedom.

Reclaiming Myself

"Knowing your own darkness is the best method for dealing with the darkness of other people" – Carl Gustav Jung

To become whole again I had to reclaim myself which essentially meant putting the pieces of the fractured puzzle that was me back together. An integral part of this process required that I address the many varying issues that were responsible for the negative thoughts and feelings that were at the heart of the fractured image that I held of myself. There were many exploratory questions that needed to be asked and answered if I was to reclaim the fragmented pieces. For example, I really needed to know how influential was my fundamental composition, was I solely the product of a past that was created from the combination of my upbringing, environment and experiences, and nothing more? Is there another me that exists below the surface of my constructed ego-self and if she does exist, who is she, what are her likes and dislikes and what does she want out of life? I asked myself who could I be if I was given the opportunity to develop into a self-possessed, non-perfectionistic and relaxed person free of the obligations, conditions and limitations that were placed on me by others and those that I had placed upon myself. What would happen if I gave myself permission to go back in time and reconnect with my young self and try to find that spark of joy that comes from the excitement at the prospect of the possibilities in life. Allowing myself the freedom of expression to unapologetically reflect my real and authentic self.

I knew that this endeavour would in no way be an easy objective to achieve, because I had to first overcome the deeply held illogical conviction that I was tainted in some way, a by-product of the long-term abuse I had experienced throughout my marriage which left me feeling unworthy and undeserving of receiving good in my life. I was also battling with varied levels of disappointment, distrust and cynicism towards certain friends and family members and their actions. This coloured the way that I looked at other people's happiness, I was both contrarily envious and at the same time in awe when I was in the presence of someone who was expressing uninhibited joy and/or laughter. I was dubious of the authenticity of their happiness thinking that they couldn't really be that happy and at the same time ironically longingly wishing that I could feel genuine happiness again to remind myself that life could be enjoyed rather than endured. My extensive research and personal therapy led me to believe that this was possible, I was tired of seeing myself as a victim or labelling myself a "survivor", because as the word suggests it sends the message to my psyche that there is always something to survive.

I have set myself on a path of exploration and rediscovery and there was no turning back, I needed to retrace my life's journey from my early childhood to the present time, searching for any distinct markers that might give me a clue as to how and why I became the person I am today. One thing was a certainty it was time to start rebuilding myself and my life and to think about how the future could look for me and my children. It was during those long days and nights throughout the renovation that became a time of deep reflection and set me on a quest for answers to the big questions particularly the "why" of everything. Why did this happen to me or did I make this happen to me through something I did or did not do? Am I being punished? What is this life about if it is only full of pain and misery? Am I insignificant in the universes scheme of things? Am I worthy of a better life? Am I destined for continued unhappiness because I made the wrong choices? My enquiring mind and my new found desire for deliverance from victimhood propelled me along my path to personal enlightenment, which amplified in voracity the more I learned. I felt empowered through the gaining of knowledge, it gave me the ability to reflect on my life without judgement and with more understanding, empathy, tolerance and acceptance for myself and others.

The major turning point for meaningful and lasting psychological and emotional growth occurred for me when I entered into private therapy while I was attending my course to become a Soul Centred Psychotherapist. It was encouraged by the course directors and it was also the best decision I had ever made in my life. I was extremely fortunate to have found a therapist that I connected with and for the next four and half years we journeyed together through the complicated labyrinth of my psyche. It was during my private therapy sessions that I began to comprehend the many different ways in which I was abused, I had mistakenly thought of abuse in simple literal terms as either verbal disparagement or physical violence and therefore easily identifiable. I did not understand the nuances and subtleties of neglect, contempt, subjugation, control and manipulation. Through exploration and analysis came understanding, illumination and clarification, I began to grasp the extent of the accumulative effects of the years of sustained emotional, psychological, verbal and physical abuse that I had undergone.

Through therapy I was able to talk about the abuse with a sense of real safety and confidence knowing that my therapist was prepared for and able to hold to what was being revealed to her and at the same time listen and accept without judgement. The retelling of particularly significant abusive events was at times distressing, I would re-live an abusive scenario and be assailed with emotions such as anxiety, shame, guilt, impotence and rage those very same emotions I had experienced when I had undergone the original abuse. However, sharing it with a compassionate and understanding therapist had helped to release some of the supressed but powerful effects that the damaging experiences inflicted on me. Together and over time we covered many of the influencing factors that impacted on my emotional, psychological and physical development such as my up-bringing which included the way I was parented, my schooling, my environment throughout my childhood and my experiences whilst growing up. We explored at great length the evolution and the consequences of my negative beliefs, my defences and my character structure, taking into consideration the bigger picture, with reference to female archetype, mythology and my direct female and male ancestral predecessors lives and their influences upon my life.

Therapy was the most precious, life-changing gift that I had ever given myself and by no means was this odyssey a "bed of roses". In fact, it was the bravest challenge I had ever undertaken, the processes alternated between being daunting, confronting, frustrating, and at times emotionally painful. However, it was also frequently and unexpectedly rewarding and enriching in the most fundamental and necessary ways. My therapist was the most amazing person I had ever encountered in my life; she was my life-line, my greatest support, my mother, my friend, my confidante and a guiding light when I felt lost. She was also not a pushover, who to my consternation habitually challenged my limiting core beliefs about life, myself, others and the world at large. She opened me up expanding my capacity to accept myself without judgment, taught me how to manage and recognise the triggers that set off my defences and most importantly she gave me the confidence to explore and surmount my deepest fears. By the time we completed our journey together I was equipped with enough confidence and the necessary tools to navigate life's challenges, my psychological and emotional load was hugely lighter and I could now envisage a positive future with more enthusiasm.

My time with this therapist ended as she had moved to a rural location to be with her family however, I continued with a new soul centred psychotherapist therapist who I called upon whenever I felt out of my depth and needed support. I learned how to ask for and receive support from others, it was a sign of a maturing psyche and my growing inner strength, I realised that by investing time and energy into looking after myself enabled me to better look after my children and myself. I also realised that there was never going to be a point in my life where I would ever stop learning and hopefully evolving.

Freedom from captivity is not simply physical separation from an abuser, it is also the attainment of emotional and psychological autonomy, wellness and wholeness. A victim will never truly be free of their abuser or the effects of the abuse itself without overcoming the issues that have bound them to their abuser in the past and perpetuated their abusive relationship. I learned that it was not enough to have left my abusive situation, although an integral step, it is by no means the only or last step to liberty. I had so much more work to do to counteract the lasting effects of the abuse which left me with lasting fears, phobias, nightmares, PTSD (post-traumatic stress disorder) and an inability to trust myself and others. True freedom only comes from within a victim's psyche and is made evident through the ability to live a healthy and happy life, free of abuse. It is also defined by their ability to enter into if they so desire their next relationship with confidence and without emotional and psychological fallout from their abusive past, ensuring that the pattern is not repeated.

Acts of abuse will always remain with a victim as long as they have a memory, however the effects of the abuse on a victim can be addressed in such a way that they lose their power to continue to further control or harm them. The degree to which wellness and wholeness may be achieved will vary with every individual and cannot be assessed or predicted, it is an individual process for each victim. There is no time limit or one specific type of therapy or therapist that provides a singular resolution. For some finding what works may include utilising combined therapies, for others it is the one therapist and one therapy, the key is to keep trying until you find who and what type of treatment feels right.

There are lasting effects from the trauma of abuse that a victim carries with them regardless of who the perpetrator is or where the abuse originated, whether it is a singular random act of abuse or ongoing abuse such as mine. The abuse does not just affect the victim that it was directed at alone, it has a ripple effect impacting on all who may be associated with the victim's plight, there is always collateral damage experienced by a victim's family, friends, witnesses, law enforcement, medical staff and case workers. These people may also suffer feeling varying degrees of impotency, guilt, shame and rage. Some family and friends may think that if they had paid more attention to the signs of abuse or if they had paid more attention to the victim's life, that they could have intervened at some point. Others who did notice and who were involved with an abusive situation in some way, who had tried to intervene, instead had their consistent attempts to help vetoed by the victim or the abuser, are often left with feelings of frustration, rage, and helplessness.

By addressing all the direct and indirect issues associated with my abuse I was able to start gathering together the splintered pieces of my psyche, slowly reassembling my fractured image back to completeness. This was definitely the most formidable task I had ever undertaken, however I realised most importantly through this process that as part of the human condition it is essential that learning and growing must never stop, and so I have resigned myself to the fact that I will always be an ongoing work in progress. To live is to evolve and so life will always present me with new challenges to overcome however, having some extra emotional and psychological tools to assist along the way is a huge bonus helping to counteract negative experiences and adverse feelings.

Hope

Throughout my childhood and teenage years, I can remember being shy despite my outward show of gregariousness, I kept my personal thoughts and feelings to myself particularly my hurts using humour as my armour. However oddly enough, there were many times when I would fight my corner displaying a fiercely determined side to my character, as friends, family and work associates would attest. My determined fighting spirit was responsible for fostering feelings of hope at times when I least expected it. This echo of hope would never allow me to completely resign myself to an unsatisfactory fate, at times driving me to keep trying at whatever it is I wanted to achieve. This contrary spirit worked both negatively and positively throughout my life, it worked against me in the sense that it compelled me to struggle to keep my dysfunctional and abusive marriage together, undergoing unnecessary heartache and abuse in order not to fail. It also paradoxically worked positively in my life as it was because of this indominable spirit that I was able to regroup, overcome adversity and forge a new life, taking steps forward with hopefulness despite my fears, uncertainties, setbacks and disappointments. No matter how frightening and exhaustive my situation became and despite the many times I had purportedly either given in or given up, there still existed a small part of me that would slowly but surely make its presence known providing me with the courage to continue the fight.

I can remember coming across the myth of "Pandoras Box" when studying goddesses and their archetypal influences on the female psyche, its duality impacted on me because it spoke of the dichotomy between hope and hopelessness. Pandora was created by the God Zeus to punish "man" because the Titan Prometheus stole the gift of fire to give to them, which Zeus believed was a gift that should only belong to the gods. She was created as the perfect woman and credited with having attributes such as wisdom, kindness, peace and generosity and she was possessed of immeasurable beauty having been moulded in the physical appearance and appeal of the Goddess Aphrodite. However, she was also bestowed with what was regarded as a fundamental flaw which was "curiosity". Epimetheus brother to Prometheus did not heed his brothers warning to be weary of any gifts given by the God Zeus and upon sighting Pandora he was instantly smitten, Epimetheus was so taken with Pandoras beauty that he asked her to marry him. On her wedding day she was gifted a box by Zeus, with the express warning that she must never open it, unfortunately her curiosity got the better of her and she opened it. As a consequence, she had inadvertently unleashed all of life's evils into the world causing untold misery and bleakness. She realised her mistake and, in her haste, to remedy her carelessness she closed the box capturing hope inside, which was an antidote offering "man" optimism as a countermeasure to the suffering. From this myth the idiom of "to open pandoras box" was created, meaning to talk about or start something that is much more complicated, unpleasant or difficult than was expected, causing possible unforeseen problems, which were better left alone.

I can relate to this myth as it eloquently mirrors one of my own life experiences, it was at a point in my life when I was being challenged to deepen my personal psychological journey, both by the directors of the psychotherapy course I was attending and also by my therapist. It seems that in order to become whole, healthy and a good psychotherapist there was much more work to be done. I needed and wanted to be whole again and knew that even though at this stage, I had gained much insight, dealt with many traumas and developed healthy coping mechanisms, that I had only chipped away at the surface layers. I was being offered another opportunity to further build my psychological and emotional robustness and elasticity, however it required that I dig much deeper and possibly open what I believed to be my own personal "can of worms" (pandoras box of memories).

I found this subsequent challenge to be considerably daunting and was quite reluctant to delve into the unknown and unpredictable because I knew that once I did, it could open me up to having to face new, unfamiliar and possibly more difficult emotional and psychological hurdles. I wasn't sure if I was prepared enough or ready to deepen the exploration to further analyse and dissect my issues, knowing I had innate anxieties and fears both conscious and unconscious to transcend. Fortunately, like Pandora, I was also possessed with a fundamentally healthy measure of curiosity, coupled with a small but determined degree of hope, which when united compelled me to continue despite my reservations. Delving into the hidden secrets of my psyche ("Pandoras box") did indeed become intensely difficult and deeply challenging, however it was also immeasurably rewarding in the long run, helping me to uncover hidden pitfalls that could have caused future impediments and unpleasantness and aiding me to grow as a potential psychotherapist. Having said that, I believed that anything worth having takes effort and therefore I knew it was never going to be an easy road to redemption and wholeness. When you start down that road of self-reflection, there is much personal work to be done if you want to peel back the layers and reveal the truth, resurrect your authentic self and change how you live your life.

Pandoras Box – The Myth

There are many written interpretations of the ancient Greek Myth of "Pandoras Box", they are all however essentially similar.

According to Greek mythology Pandora was considered to be the first woman on earth. She was created by Zeus who wanted to punish the Titan Prometheus brother to Epimetheus for stealing fire and giving it to man, a gift that Zeus considered only worthy of possession by the Gods.

He created her so that she would be a temptation that Epimetheus could not resist, hence he asked the lesser Gods and Goddesses to gift her with attributes such as beauty, kindness, peace, generosity and health. Aphrodite bestowed on her a feminine beauty equal to her own, Athena gave her wisdom, however Hermes was ordered to teach her to be stubborn and curious.

As a wedding present Zeus gave Pandora a box, telling her that it contained special gifts from the Gods but that she was never permitted to open the box. Unfortunately, her innate curiosity got the better of her and she opened the box unleashing all of life's miseries and evils in the world, realising her mistake she closed the box trapping hope inside.

According to one version of the myth, by trapping hope inside and out of reach it fulfilled Zeus's ultimate desire to punish those who disobeyed the Gods.

In other versions of the myth, hope is the last to escape from the box, providing opportunity for those who disobey with the possibility for redemption, or that hope is the antidote to malady, misery and evil.

This story has become an idiom over time with the meaning "to open pandoras box" is to start something that will cause many detrimental and unforeseen consequences. The modern equivalent is "opening a can of worms".

Redemption

The formal meaning of the word redemption is; regaining possession of something in exchange for payment.

For myself and my children our redemption was gaining the right to live a life in freedom, peace, and safety, our payment was the trials and tribulations we had to undergo in order to attain the life we wanted and the heartache and suffering that accompanied it. My personal redemption was twofold, the first and biggest reward that made everything I went through and struggled for worthwhile was watching my children flourish and grow to become whole human-beings in an environment that was free of discord, oppression, and instability. I worked hard and fought for their freedom and happiness and I believe I achieved this despite my ex-husband's unwelcome intrusions into our lives. It was by no means easy, parenting never is but I knew it had to better than the alternative which for myself and my children was to live under adverse dysfunctional conditions.

There is no such thing as a perfect family dynamic, each unit is shaped by their unique experiences as a group and by each individual in that group. It is established by a combination of their genealogy, religious and political beliefs, environmental and cultural influences, economic circumstances and by their family history and therefore made unique by these definitive factors. As a result, every family and every individual in that family will have their own set of challenges all of whom will possess a distinctive combination of complexities and idiosyncrasies. Today's family units are far cry from the predominant traditional nuclear family unit's characteristic of the nineteen fifties and sixties which comprised of mother (female), father (male) and children. In the mix now there are, step families, married/unmarried partner families with the same or opposite sex, adoptive/foster families and families where the children are raised by relatives, each dynamic possessing a distinctive set of advantages and challenges. It is also quite common to find children being reared in single parent families and even though they are generally found to be economically disadvantaged, this does not necessarily equate to being disadvantaged psychologically and/or emotionally. Having one reasonably adjusted parent with "good enough" parenting skills is better than having two maladaptive individuals who are co-parenting through their dysfunctional relationship.

In fact, I will go so far as to say that in retrospect after having been faced with the same challenges that coupled parents had faced with their children's physical, emotional and psychological development, particularly during the children's teenage years with schooling and the dreaded social passage towards young adulthood (alcohol, drugs, bullying, sex, dating and parties). That we as a single parent family unit managed to thrive finding our own brand of happiness and contentment despite our challenges, living free of the adversities and constraints that would have been present had I stayed in my decaying marriage. I believe that my continued effort to progressively learn more about myself was, and still remains the key to increasing the possibility of success. I felt it essential to maintain a concerted effort to continue to develop and grow intellectually, emotionally and psychologically. This not only sustained and cultivated my individual growth, but also helped to monitor and address my own existing or possible future personal issues and improved my capacity to be a better person and a better parent.

The second taste of redemption that I received that validated all my past adversity was a much more private reward in the form of the attainment of my own personal individual freedom that allowed me to thrive and grow. It was the most amazing feeling to be free, I could breathe again without the constant anxiety that used to thrum in the background of my mind imbuing all my thoughts, decisions and actions like white noise. I was able to make decisions based on my own priorities, needs and goals without having them overshadowed with guilt, shame, anxiety or fear. This feeling of freedom that most people take for granted was not experienced immediately post gaining liberty from my abusive situation. It took me years to adapt to all the subtle nuances that embody the feeling of autonomy that the word freedom suggests. The procurement of freedom from the effects of long-term abuse is an individual odyssey for all victims of abuse and I was no exception to that rule. My journey towards full autonomy was layered with unforeseen psychological and emotional complexities, creating obstacles that I was forced to address as they became apparent in my life. However, every advancement that I achieved throughout this

116

process contributed to my rehabilitation and transformation, I regained precious lost parts of myself helping me to re-establish my individual identity.

I did not realise how rigid, inhibited and supressed I had become until I was free from the oppression, restriction and subjugation that was imposed on me by my flawed relationship and by my own psychological dysfunction. I was not only trapped in abominable circumstances by my abusive partner but also by my own limiting beliefs as well as some maladaptive defences, and my negatively orientated ingrained core character structure (refer to book one). I had to learn to allow myself to be healthily spontaneous and unconstrained, to think and act without the concerns that usually besiege my decision-making processes. This was something new for me because it meant letting go of some of the unyielding control that I believed had protected me throughout my adult life. By giving myself permission to participate in unplanned and impromptu activities, I was able to recapture some of the childlike feelings of joyous buoyancy that comes with the carefree abandon of youth. My "young self" or as some of you may refer to as your "inner child" was repressed for so long that even embracing the smallest liberties had a powerfully positive impact on my psyche. Having the freedom to be able to make what may seem to others as the smallest inconsequential choices, was a luxury to me such as choosing the type of food I would buy at the supermarket without the strictures imposed on me by my husband's dietary dictates and time constraints. Being completely unconstrained and/or spontaneous is something I still struggle with today and although I do feel as if I am much better with embracing and expressing my authentic and natural self, I am certain there is still room for further expansion.

Redemption is a gift given for perseverance in the face of adversity and I am still today at times surprised by the new and unexpected experiences of redemption that arise as I challenge previously held internal emotional and psychological boundaries to discover dormant aspects of myself. It is a continued source of validation regardless of the hardship, struggle or length of time it takes to overcome misfortune and suffering, the rectification and reparation is a reward that far outweighs the harrowing journey to get there. It is always possible to stretch your capacity to achieve a more fulfilling experience of life, by challenging outmoded beliefs, patterns of behaviour and personality traits that hinder, hide or supress your authenticity. It is the act of holding a mirror up to yourself with the intention to discover what lurks beyond the ego-ideal you hold of yourself and acknowledge that there is another you below the surface. It can only happen if you give yourself permission to accept without judgment those parts of yourself that you disapprove of in others and by opening yourself up to the idea of review, rehabilitation and/or transformation.

It seems that during the first part of our lives, we are not given the choice as to who we are to be parented by and therefore have little control over how we are shaped, leaving us at the mercy of our upbringing and our circumstances. However, in the second part of our lives we are provided with the facility and the opportunity to change, repair or redirect the trajectory of our lives if we so desire, we have the capacity to make our own choices. It is extremely beneficial to take the time to reflect over your upbringing and early life experiences to alter the behaviours and thought patterns that have been taught to you but no longer serve you. These are the beliefs, thoughts and behaviours that have become physically, emotionally and psychologically obsolete or redundant, that are now working against you, repressing your authenticity and prohibiting you from advancing and flourishing.

There comes a time in your life when you need to evaluate what is good and positive in your life and what is not. Reviewing and amending your beliefs around fundamental matters such as intimacy, sex, love, friendship, money, work and religion. If you are feeling apprehensive, dissatisfied and/or deeply unhappy and are not where you want to be, perhaps you have chosen the wrong profession, career path, educational direction or you are in a declining or adverse intimate relationship, life style or friendship group wishing you could change your circumstances. The time to do it is always now, no matter how difficult or daunting the prospect of change is, it all starts with one small simple step and that is to take the time to consider (imagine) the changes you would like to see happen and what that would look and feel like. There is absolutely no need to suffer unnecessarily if you have a choice not to, contrary to what some spiritual and religious dogma is known to advocate. It does not matter who you are or how old you are, if things are not working for you then perhaps it is time to examine why you are unhappy or discontent. Ask yourself the question who is telling you that you cannot change your circumstances, is it a voice in your head, or is it an external voice that perhaps has their own interests in keeping you from changing your life.

Becoming Whole

My journey towards wholeness started the moment I chose to truly reflect on my life, who I was and how I was living that life and then subsequently wanting to change it.

Every woman whether she is conscious of it or not endeavours to traverse her own unique path towards wholeness and the union of mind, body, and intuition (instinctual wisdom). She will have her own personal heroine's odyssey to navigate with particular challenges to meet and overcome, unfortunately for some it will be a more difficult journey than for others, such is the randomness of life. She will strive to rectify the disunion between her inner masculine and inner feminine that were created by conditions beyond her control, but that formed part of her physical, emotional and psychological identity. The disparity between her inner masculine and inner feminine is initiated in her early developmental years and then cemented into her psyche in the following years through her teens and beyond. This is something that she cannot avoid and is a negative by-product of the patriarchal society in which she was raised. It is the culmination of a series of influences such as the type of parenting she received, her economic, environmental and sociological (religious and cultural) conditions and her personal experiences while growing up. We are the sum of many parts; each part plays an integral role influencing our inner workings and outward display of emotion and behaviour which in turn reflects what we believe to be our identity or ego-ideal of ourselves.

The most integral part of my journey was in fact righting the psychological misconceptions that I had developed in my early formative years and which were consolidated in my later years, through my maladaptive marriage. The moment I started meaningful self-reflection, I had triggered the onset of a powerful process; one I could not walk away from and which was the catalyst that propelled me toward a better life. I had woken up from a deep coma, I was sleepwalking through life letting myself be led rather than leading, I was a puppet at the mercy of my maladaptive beliefs. Realisations can be both painful and enlightening, nonetheless they are definitely a necessary act of growth whether welcomed or not. I had to face many confronting truths about myself, my relationships and my life as a whole throughout my metamorphic journey. The most difficult realisation that I had encountered was the devastating truth that my whole life appeared to be fictitious and therefore insubstantial. My house of cards collapsed because it was built on unrealities, lies, false projections and held together by delusion, it was a structure built on fragile foundations, inevitably destined for suffering and adversity.

It became imperative that I change who I was and the way I was living my life, not realising at the time that just by the act of contemplating the changes I desired to see happen, I had instigated natures transformative processes. I had unconsciously unlocked the portal to begin taking the necessary evolutionary steps that needed to occur in order to create the future I had envisioned. It did not matter whether the steps I took were right or wrong or the length of time it took to make them, and even though my resolve wavered at various times, my intention remained steadfast, which is what brought me to where I wanted to be in the end. Initially I did not actually know what that end would look like, all I knew was what I thought and felt I needed and wanted which was to live in a safe and peaceful environment, one that would be interspersed with a good kind of excitement. This included freedom from anxiety, fear and uncertainty and to be given the opportunity to be me and I wanted those same things for my children. Being certain of and knowing what you need and want are requisite when contemplating your future, however you don't have to have all the details mapped out. Determinedly holding to your end goal (the bigger picture) helps to strengthen your conscious intention creating an impetus for change.

Freeing Myself from Past Trauma

"One who looks outside dreams; one who looks inside awakes" – Carl Gustav Jung

The biggest part of becoming whole again was freeing myself from the past effects of trauma that were debilitating my attempts to lead a normal and healthy present life. Healing myself through therapy was the ultimate act of self-reclamation that allowed me to truly be free of psychological and emotional suffering, disharmony and perpetual anxiety. It was responsible for generating feelings of inner equilibrium and peace, providing me with the confidence with which to manage present day challenges and the tools to face possible future adversity. It helped me to reconcile injurious past events and resolve residual feelings of grief, resentment and rage while fostering feelings of contentment, optimism and a general feeling of well-being. I had made strong connections with my body which allowed me to feel a more expansive and healthy range of emotions through addressing and overcoming issues of depression, dissociation, negative thought patterns and feelings of unworthiness, failure and inadequacy. I learned to listen to what my body was telling me and to trust my innate intuition which helped to bring my physical, emotional and psychological body into alignment and harmony. By challenging and subsequently discarding my negatively driven core beliefs which were responsible for driving my defences and forming my character structure, I was able to develop a new set of beliefs that worked to serve me in a positive and uplifting manner.

The general pervasive unconscious belief that I had intrinsically failed in some way had played a substantial role in undermining my self-confidence and my achievements throughout my life. It fostered deep feelings of inferiority and defectiveness. I learned to recognise, understand and relent with regard to my habituated inclination towards the attainment of perfectionism, which was one of the negative ways in which I defended against feelings of failure. It was one of the major underlying issues that needed to be addressed in order for me to move forward in a positive way in my life. Thankfully I adopted a new belief that provided me with great personal relief, I realised that doing my best was actually "good enough" regardless of what other people thought and irrespective of any externally based standards. This new belief acted to liberate me from my self-imposed unrelenting standards that would never allow me to feel content with my endeavours and achievements or allow me to realise a level of acceptance or success.

I believe it is essential to work with past trauma to bring it to heel or it will always arise at inopportune moments in your life to sabotage or undermine your present-day happiness and/or attempts to move forward. Unresolved traumatic issues are like a disease that when left unchecked continue to fester becoming a persistent primary cause of physical illness as well as being responsible for needless psychological and emotional torment and suffering. These underlying issues will most definitely affect every aspect of your life, limiting your capacity to feel real contentment, happiness, joy and peacefulness. It will hinder your ability to attain whatever goals you may have set yourself and be responsible for cultivating negative feelings such as failure, unworthiness, guilt, shame, sadness, apathy, discontent, anxiety and depression. My personal measure of wholeness is defined as a collaboration of many diverse factors coming together, obviously reclamation, redemption, and healing from the past effects of trauma were integral key factors forming an extensive part of becoming healthy and whole. However, there were several other significant life-changing events that were essential elements that added to my attainment of wholeness, these included, overcoming inherent and debilitating shame, completing my course to become a Soul Centred Psychotherapist, reuniting with my family after twenty years apart and of course writing about my personal journey with abuse.

Overcoming Shame

"Shame is a soul eating emotion" – Carl Gustav Jung

One of the most insidiously poisonous and incapacitating emotions that I had to face and overcome was my deep-seeded feeling of innate shame. It was through personal therapy that I came to understand that the burdensome shame I was carrying was not just my own but also that of other people. There is a healthy level of shame needed to help human-beings temper their wrongful and/or hurtful behaviour towards others and society at large, enabling them to co-exist in harmony. However, this emotion can become troublesome and deeply oppressive for those of us who are carrying an unhealthy overcompensation of this devasting emotion, causing us to live less than adequate and limiting lives. The overcompensation is usually comprised of a combination of other peoples and/or previous generations disowned (cast off or denied) or displaced (shifted or transferred) shame. Those that do not own their shame tend to project it outwards onto others who are non-deserving but none the less become the victims of someone else's shameful actions.

During my therapy I had gradually peeled back the layers of shame I was carrying only to discover that it was more complex than I understood it to be. Not only was I hampered by my own personal shame I was also carrying on my shoulders other people's shame, a combination of my fathers, my husbands, my predecessors and even to some degree that of the Serbian forces that committed war crimes during the war of independence in the 1990's in the former Yugoslavia. As strange as that may sound, I was deeply affected by the atrocities being committed by the warring factions during that terrible war even though I was not born or raised in Serbia. I can remember being acutely affected by a poignant image of a woman who was sitting in a field that held a backdrop of the effects of bombing from enemy forces. She was garbed in all black, with a mantle covering her head and shoulders a common uniform for women who were in mourning, she was elderly perhaps in her seventies. There was a look of complete and utter shock that seemed to have arrested her face, the look in her eyes spoke of the devastation that she must have witnessed and the grief from her loss. Her posture was that of a human spirit who was experiencing feelings of profound defeat and hopelessness. She left an indelible imprint on me emotionally and psychologically; I felt her pain and I also felt the shame that the perpetrators of the acts abuse on the innocent were choosing to ignore. Those participating in the atrocities were descendants of the Serb nation that my father hailed from and even though I felt no kinship with these people I still carried on a deeply unconscious level, their repudiated shame.

On a more personally intimate level I experienced shame that was a direct result of my own misconceived short-comings and feelings of inadequacy combined with the disowned shame of those influential people closest to me. I carried the burden of the shame that my father and my husband refused to acknowledge, something that is considered to be an idiosyncratic aspect of those who are afflicted with narcissistic disorders. Their character traits are such that it does not permit them to experience emotions such as shame or guilt as it would undermine the ego-ideals they hold of themselves and it would also curtail their uncaring, self-serving activities. As a result, they project these unwanted feelings onto others, however it is more often than not those who are closest to them who will unconsciously carry the weight of their unacknowledged shame, to which I had unknowingly fallen prey to. Unfortunately, this is not something innocent victims have a choice in and it will undoubtedly add an emotional and psychological heaviness to an individual's life that they will be unaware of.

However, when "shame" is given its duly respectful recognition and acknowledgment through therapeutic intervention. It can be addressed in such a way so as to dispel its harmful affect and return it to its rightful owner (the original perpetrator/s of the shameful acts) regardless of how far back in the family tree that needs to go. It seems that as human-beings we do not realise that any acts that we commit today good or bad have the capacity to affect those lineal generations that follow us in an archetypal energetic sort of way. In other words, those of us who disacknowledge the emotion of shame and/or guilt while committing crimes of abuse today will cast a shadow that effects the innocent in the current generation and the generations that follow. Working through and exposing the varying levels of shame I carried within my psychological and emotional body was both immensely difficult and equally liberating at the same time, freeing me of excess and unnecessary conscious and unconscious torment and suffering.

Becoming a Psychotherapist

Striving for and completing my course to become a Soul Centred Psychotherapist was another stepping stone to wholeness for me, I had challenged and overcome one of my biggest psychological hurdles which was the innate feeling of failure that I had unconsciously carried throughout much of my life. The core belief that I was or had failed in some intrinsic way and would therefore inevitably fail no matter what I attempted to accomplish or how hard I tried would quite possibly have been responsible for unconsciously sabotaging every achievement I had ever attained. It always left me with the feeling that I hadn't done enough or I had done it wrongly despite the seeming show of success. My innate fear of failure had been significantly instrumental in keeping me attached to my abuser and my abusive situation. It was responsible for driving me to continually try to make a success out of our dysfunctional relationship and it was utilised by my abuser to keep me from realising my true value. Early on in our relationship he had discerned that I was unsure of myself and that I had possessed feelings of self-doubt and I believe he made sure to capitalise on this perceived vulnerability by further reinforcing the negative belief I held of myself at every opportune occasion.

While attending my psychotherapy course and as a student this negative core belief was repeatedly challenged by the demands of the course itself and by one of my teachers who became aware of this issue when asking me to participate in a public demonstration (in class) of the skills we had learned. Public speaking was a natural part of the course training and yet it was the most intimidating hurdle for me, filling me with a deep sense of dread causing me to freeze up, robbing me of the ability to speak at all. Whenever I was asked to put into practice what I had learned in front of a group of fellow students, I would react like a deer caught in headlights activating my "fight, flight or freeze" response. This was because I lacked confidence and did not believe or trust in what I had learned which triggered my fear of failing, causing overwhelming feelings of shame to claim my body and rob me of the fundamental capacity to communicate or to function (I dissociated). My instructor was the first person to take note of this issue within me having been a witness to it first hand in our classroom setting, however I was not the only one in our class with this issue and so he supported each of us to learn to acknowledge, understand and deal with this underlying issue. The course itself paradoxically provided the antidote to our plight through its education on the causes that cultivate feelings of failure in human-beings and at the same time he did not relent but continued to challenge those of us who harboured feelings of failure and inadequacy to step up to the task in order to complete the course.

Finishing the course to become a Soul Centred Psychotherapist was one of the most deeply rewarding achievements in my life. It provided me with feelings of immeasurable personal confidence, it resurrected my self-esteem and it nurtured the feeling of being of value. This replaced my original negative feelings of being inadequate and insignificant, I felt useful again, I realised that I had something to contribute to society besides being a mother, I could be of help to other victims of abuse. Becoming a psychotherapist gave me a new life purpose and it also dawned on me that this is what I was meant to be doing, it felt right. A prevailing feeling of rightness and contentment filled me, my innate wisdom was telling me that this is what it feels like to be a part of the rhythm of life. I was no longer floundering around in deep water or fighting against the pull of the current of uncertainty, but rather I had finally relaxed into her flow. I had discovered a life's purpose which was both nurturing for others and personally deeply fulfilling for me, I had also created circumstances and a purpose in which I could flourish, grow, and build healthy self-esteem.

Reuniting with My Family

I did not anticipate that when I reunited with my family that I would be faced with such a contradiction of emotion; it was a combination of being complex and difficult at times and alternately poignant and rewarding at other times. It had been twenty years since I had seen or spoken to my parents, four siblings and their partners and I had not yet met my nieces and nephew. This was yet another personal formidably daunting expedition into unchartered emotional and psychological territory for me, I was not sure how we were going to breach the chasm that the separation of time had created and I was anxious about how all the individual family members themselves were going to respond to us (my children and I). I was also highly apprehensive about how we would fit into each other's lives in the future and whether we could put the past behind us without recrimination and resentment or would one or more of them wish to rehash past issues, something I was not ready to do with them. It took me some time but I finally realised that there would probably never be a perfect time for this reunion to transpire, nor was there ever going to be a time when I was going to feel confident or prepared enough to meet with them.

My eldest brother and I had been periodically communicating by telephone for about three years after my initial separation from my ex-husband however, I had resisted reuniting with my whole family. This was for several reasons firstly, because I still harboured fears that my ex-husband would become retaliatory towards me and them if I reunited with them straight away. He frequently and quite vocally continued to disparage and malign their character to me and my children post our divorce, and because I was still trying to establish boundaries with him, it was another source of contention I could not deal with. Secondly, I had issues with my father that had been left unresolved since my disconnect from the family twenty years earlier and I did not feel that I was ready to address those issues while still having to deal with my adversarial ex-husband. Nevertheless, the time finally did come when I felt it was safe enough to reconnect with the whole family and so through my brother, we had organised to meet each other for Sunday lunch at my parents' house. To say I was anxious was an understatement, however even though I appeared to my children to be outwardly calm, I was in fact internally extremely apprehensive. I did not realise how truly disconcerted I had become that day until while on our road trip to the lunch I almost caused a major collision with several other vehicles. This was because I had failed to stop at a major intersection where a red light was flashing, very nearly driving myself and the children into the middle of a major eight lane arterial highway, lucky for all of us that my children noticed and shouted for me to stop.

When we arrived at my parents' home, we were warmly welcomed by all, this was followed by a lovely lunch prepared by my mother which was delicious reminding me how much I had missed her home cooking. We had a lovely time getting to know each other again, naturally there were some awkward moments interrupting the flow of conversation, which were tactically smoothed over by my brother in order to preserve the integrity of this first get-together. From this point on things just got easier, the children and I integrated into the family and they into mine, we became a major part of each other's lives. There of course had to be some compromise on both sides, time and life's challenges and experiences had changed all of us as individuals and as a family unit. We like all families had our group dynamics based on our idiosyncratic history and the interpersonal relationships that had developed as a result. However, the individual and group dynamics that were established between us prior to the twenty-year separation no-longer applied to me, I had been changed irrevocably by my experiences. We had to work to establish new boundaries that did not exist in my previous relationships with them, we had to make allowances for changed personalities on both sides.

Initially I never intended to tell my family of the abuse I had undergone during my marriage or why I had not tried to connect with them during the interim three years post my divorce. This was for good reason as I was deeply concerned that one of them may react in an outraged manner and decide that they would confront my ex-husband and/or there was also the possibility that they may speak about it to others, who might leak information. I was extremely worried that it would get back to him, which could compromise the tentative safety that I had created for myself and my children from my ex-husband, who would likely retaliate against me or my family if he felt even remotely slighted, threatened or if heard that his character was being maligned publicly. It was an unspoken understanding between all of us (my family and myself) that we never discuss my ex-husband so as not to derail the fragile new relationship we were all trying to forge. I had been profoundly changed by my experiences and was no longer the naïve and malleable daughter that my father and mother may remember. I was in the midst of developing a strong sense of self and could not be easily led, manipulated or coerced into doing anything I did not want to do or sharing personal information if I chose not to. My Father possessed a forceful personality with strong narcissistic tendencies, he was opinionated and tended to speak his mind without regard to others feelings or opinions. I did not want him to perceive me as the "prodigal daughter" returning home ashamed and defeated and at the same time, I was aware that knowing him it certainly may appear to him that my homecoming might bear a resemblance to that parable.

He was extremely overcome with emotion when he first saw me and could not speak, I on the other had been taken back by his somewhat diminutive appearance having remembered him as being larger than life in personality and physicality. Nevertheless, we overcame our awkwardness over the next few months to develop a grudging respect and acceptance of each other's changed personalities. My mother on the other hand did not appear to be the least bit daunted by our reunion and the two of us settled into a relationship with ease, even though we never spoke about my twenty-year separation. She was thrilled to have me back in her life and especially the prospect of two more grandchildren to spoil and she proceeded to shower us all with her attention and love. I developed differing relationships with each of my siblings, we were changed human-beings and as is always the case in big families you can become closer to one or two in particular. My sister and I had formed the strongest bond since our reunion, she was only seventeen years old when I married and prior to that we experienced the usual childhood rivalry that occurs between two sisters sharing a room and a wardrobe.

To say we are complex family is an understatement, even before I was married and moved out of home, we had significant familial inter-personal conflicts, the result of seven differing personalities each of us quite vocal and opiniated. We could argue about anything and everything, our dinner table was a time when we all came together and if anyone had something to say they certainly said it, we usually all spoke at once and over the top of each other. Food was a big part of our lives and we ate with relish while discussing or arguing over whatever was the topic du-jour at the time, anyone watching would have thought there was a mini war going on at the dinner table. This was our norm we might have yelled in our attempt to ensure we were heard over one another and it may appear as if we were having a major row and even though on occasion we were, there also existed a strong familial bond. This bond was unspoken and was made evident whenever an outsider attempted to target one of the members of our family unit with any ill intent, they would receive the full defensive force of the whole family. We protected our own from outsiders and despite the in-house conflict we were quite a formidable family, we fought just as much as we laughed. We were a family that consistently entertained and socialised and so our home was always full of people, there was either left-overs in the fridge or hot food cooking on the stove, and in the background was the ever-present sounds of some of the greatest singers of all time, Martin, Sinatra, and Nat King Cole.

In the past I can remember that we gave each other hell in the sense that we were very much in each other's business and taking the mickey out of each other was a given, "stirring" (making fun) was a big part of our familial composition. Whether you liked it or not, or whether you were in the mood for it or not you were "stirred" (made fun of) and so we each had to develop the ability to stand up to it and to give back as good as we got. As a result, we all developed a sense of humour, we had the capacity to laugh with each other and were able to find the humourous side in the many constant ups and downs in our lives regardless of the seriousness of the experience. I was reminded of this when I reunited with my family, my siblings and I reminisced over remembered significant anecdotal incidents and the many pranks that we played on each other and our parents throughout our adolescence. The most difficult challenge I had encountered in my reunion with my family was re-establishing a relationship with my father. It seems that we had both engaged in an unspoken truce of sorts wherein neither of us spoke about anything other than my children and their lives growing up. I was careful to edit out major parts of my personal life with him, as I didn't feel I could trust him enough to share any personal painful details with him. This new relationship had to be on my terms or not at all as I still harboured some residual unresolved disappointment and discontent towards him for his betrayal of my trust twenty years earlier.

My father possessed a character that could at times be alternately proud, stubborn and selfish and I knew he had little capacity for self-reflection. I believed him to be incapable of true self-reproach or be able to take absolute responsibility for any wrongdoings in his life, using self-serving rationalisations to justify his actions. I understood this about him when I reunited with my family, I knew I would never get an apology from him, although I secretly hoped that there was some small possibility that at some point in our future there would be some kind of gesture from him of real conciliation for his past transgressions towards me. Having said that, I also understood that he possessed emotional and psychological limitations with origins that reached far back into his own maladaptive childhood and subsequent life experiences which shaped him in a way that made honest reflection for him improbable, he was too old and set in his ways to ever change. I was under no illusion that that my father and I would ever be able to wholly breach the rift between us to my satisfaction and had come to terms with this fact. However, I was content to make peace and reconcile with him, so that my children could experience their grandfather, grandmother and my siblings and some of the merriment, playfulness and humour that is a fundamental part of my family's framework.

There does not exist a family that does not possess some type of dysfunction that had likely played a role in shaping its participants whether the participants are consciously aware of it or not. Our family is no different, I have learned to accept this and approach the relationships within my family with a clearer understanding of our interpersonal dynamics. I have learned to set emotional, psychological and physical boundaries whenever I deem it necessary, respecting others point of view and protecting mine. I am not the same person that walked back into their lives, I was not able to and also did not in any way want to fulfill the role that I played in my family previous to my twenty-year separation. I realised that they as individuals had grown and changed, although their group inter-dependant relationships had not altered, I however, came back into their fold a fundamentally changed person from the one they remembered. There were adjustments that had to be made on both sides in order for us to become cohesive again and even though the process at times was deeply challenging we managed to overcome our differences to reconnect on a genuine and much more meaningful level than our past relationships. This however, did by no means preclude us from having inhouse disagreements and petty arguments that any large family whose members are strongly opiniated and stubborn would engage in.

Breaking the Silence

"The privilege of a life-time is to become who you truly are" – Carl Gustav Jung

Unfortunately, I was made aware of the harsh realities of life having my innocence slowly but systematically stripped away from me throughout my relationship by my abusive partner. This dysfunctional relationship spanned a period of three decades in which I endured many different forms of abuse and to which I believed myself to be held captive. Through the telling of my story, I feel as if I have torn down the barbed wire fence that was keeping me silent, this fence was an invisible psychological boundary that prohibited me from speaking my truth and prevented me from completing my personal journey to wholeness. One of the biggest obstacles I had faced throughout my life was not having a voice, something I found to have been prescribed to me by the patriarchal society in which I grew up and which was also unintentionally endorsed by my parents, who in turn were taught by their predecessors. I can only conjecture from the little I know about my female ancestors, surmising this was not just my story but also that of my mothers and I imagine many of the females on both my mothers and father's ancestral line of descent. I believe I am one of many women in a long line of women who have been made prisoner, subjugated by their silence, whose authenticity, freedom of speech and liberty has been curtailed by their husbands, parents, families, religions, cultures, social structures and societal dispositions and rules.

When I look back over my family history at the circumstances under which my mother was raised and those women before her, it seems that they were victims of traditional patriarchal societies, ruled by men and influenced by archaic, male dominated religious dogma. They were conditioned to adhere to rules restricting their natural inclinations, prohibiting them from having their innate needs met and required to be submissive to their male counterparts. This was never directly taught to me but more something I learned from witnessing my parent's relationships and their interactions with their contemporaries. It was a very big part of the subliminal messages that the society in which I was raised had espoused, advocating the belief that as women we were secondary in every way to our male counterparts. Overcoming my own ingrained strongly held unconscious and conscious beliefs was the key that unlocked the cell door to the self-imposed incarceration I placed on myself. These negatively held beliefs played a significant role in keeping me from claiming my freedom from a reprehensible relationship and robbed me from knowing or expressing my true and authentic self.

I have claimed back my right to be, live and speak without reserve and without fear of criticism or judgment, I am no longer a hostage to others peoples limited thinking and have given myself permission to express myself with genuineness and self-assurance. Writing this book has been extremely cathartic for me as I have breached the ultimate taboo that I had placed on myself which was to speak frankly and honestly about my experience of abuse, something I never thought I could or would ever do. It has taken me over three decades to speak my truth, I have crossed a once forbidden personal boundary through the telling of my intimate journey with domestic abuse with the sincere hope that I have reached those of you who may benefit from my hard-earned understandings. For myself I have learned and grown throughout the process of writing this book but most importantly It has provided me with the last missing piece of the puzzle that is me. A piece I didn't know was missing until I completed this book, it gave me back the power to speak with candour, completing my restoration to wholeness of spirit.

Betrayal by the Masculine

Male dominancy is one of the earliest known, most pervasive forms of abuse in human history.

One of the archetypal Greek myths that reflects quite poignantly an aspect of my personal journey is the myth of Persephone and Hades. In this myth Persephone is used as a bartering tool by her father the God Zeus, his aim is to gain an alliance with his brother the powerful underworld God Hades. Together they plan Persephone's abduction and subsequent marriage to Hades without her or mother's knowledge or consent. Hades does kidnap Persephone taking her to the underworld where he rules, he is smitten by her and tries his best to persuade her to want to stay. He showers her with gifts, creates a beautiful garden for her own personal use and he builds her a throne so that she may rule beside him. However, Persephone desperately misses her mother the Goddess Demeter and her life above ground, so she takes a stand against Zeus by refusing to eat. In the meantime, Demeter in her grief and despair is searching the earth over for her beloved daughter and as a result the earth to which she was the patroness/overseer was being neglected. The masses were starving they were pleading with Zeus and the other Gods for aid, in response to their cries for help Zeus had sent a messenger (Hermes) into the Underworld with an edict ordering Hades to return Persephone to her mother.

Hades had to comply to the request but was not prepared to willingly give her up, so he came up with a plan to trick them all. One of the rules of the underworld is that if you taste the food of the underworld, you must remain there forever. Persephone who had been starving herself during her stay in the underworld was tricked by Hades into eating a handful of pomegranate seeds before she left to go back to her family. She was reunited with her mother and heartily welcomed by the people as she was the bringer of the season of Spring, returning the earth to a regenerative state. However, Hades came above ground to claim Persephone back demanding that his wife be returned to live with him as she had eaten fruit from the underworld. Demeter the Goddess of grain and agriculture became enraged, refusing to relinquish her daughter to Hades, declaring that she would retaliate if her daughter is taken from her by neglecting the earth, causing famine and pestilence until all humans die. Zeus not wanting to make an enemy of Hades, but also not wanting to alienate his consort the goddess Demeter, made the ruling decision that Persephone will spend half the year with Hades in the underworld (autumn and winter) and the other half of the year above ground with Demeter her mother (spring and summer).

As a psychological archetype, this myth can represent a metaphor for a loveless marriage, engineered by two heads of a family wishing an advantageous alliance through the union of marriage via their progeny. This is represented in the real world showcased by the many ruling families throughout history who have married their sons and daughters to other similar ruling nations creating strategic alliances that will benefit them without regard to their children's own desires. They are simply pawns to be bartered at the mercy of their progenitors. Arranged marriages are still occurring today, they are often either a business arrangement between rich and powerful families or simply as some cultures and religions dictate a "father's prerogative" to autocratically choose a son in-law or daughter in-law for their offspring. This myth also sends a powerful message about the profound betrayal of trust by a father to his daughter. In this myth Persephone must face the unpleasant truth that someone who she has placed her blind faith in and whom she loves and admires has used her for his own selfish purposes without remorse. She had become a pawn to be used callously by her father who has had her own possible desire to marry for love with someone of her own choosing disregarded. Imagine her shock and despair when she found out it was her father who relegated her to a loveless marriage with a stranger in a place that precluded her from ever seeing her home and her mother again.

This myth may also represent a "psychological metaphor" for a woman who finds herself involuntarily or inadvertently visiting the "underworld," a consequence brought on by a real-life event. She may have been taken by force either kidnapped, sold into slavery or by an arranged marriage, or it may have been by choice wherein she voluntarily but unwittingly entered into an abusive relationship. Either way she is compelled in a sense to take a journey into the "underworld" or rather the unconscious aspects of her psyche, wherein she will have to face the negative influencing dysfunctional elements of her own psychological composition. The myth shows us how a young woman in her trusting naivete can be snatched away from the beauty of her innocent world into the darkness of the underworld by a trickster whose reasons are purely self-serving. She has become a sacrifice on the altar of injustice, her choices are no longer hers, here she will have to fight for her physical, emotional and psychological survival. It is here I draw a parallel to my father and my husband who both used me as an instrument to fulfil their egoic agendas, both engaging in an unconscious battle of wills for supremacy over the right to ownership over my autonomy, however my husband won out in the end, taking me down to the underworld where he resided.

According to the myth Persephone spent half her time in the darkness of the underworld and half her time in the sunlight of the world above, like Persephone perhaps it is part of the human female condition to exist in both worlds until she can evolve enough to find her own resolution. She may have to traverse and conquer the challenges of the underworld in order to attain her personal growth and transformation. Could the myth be a metaphor reflecting every heroine's journey and that she must travel between the two disparate worlds facing adversity in her quest to find her individual strength, purpose, authenticity and freedom.

The Myth of Hades
and Persephone

The Greek Myth of Hades and Persephone has several versions, all with slightly different connotations but essentially the fundamentals of the story remain the same, some say she fell in love with Hades, others say she despised her marriage to Hades.

It starts with Zeus, the King of the gods who was brother to Demeter the Goddess of Harvest and Fertility. Demeter was also Zeus's consort, together they conceived a child whom they named Persephone a Goddess known for her kind-heartedness and great beauty.

Demeter loved her daughter deeply, protecting her and keeping her close to her side, innocent and naïve to the ways of the world.

One day Hades, the God of the underworld and Zeus's brother, came up from the underworld and happened to catch sight of Persephone playing with a group of nymphs in a field. At once he was struck by her beauty and her tenderness towards the nymphs, deciding that he would ask his brother Zeus for her hand in marriage.

Zeus was only too pleased to give his consent as he considered Hades to be the most stable, powerful, and richest of all the Gods, however Zeus knew that Demeter would never sanction this marriage and so he conspired with Hades to help him to kidnap Persephone.

One day when Persephone wandered away from her protective escort of nymphs and into a field, she came across a beautiful flower (narcissus), as she reached to pluck one, the earth opened-up. Hades appeared charging forth on a chariot pulled by black horses, he snatched Persephone up before she could scream and plunged back into the underworld, the earth closing instantly.

While in the underworld Persephone was treated with kindness and respect, Hades had showered her with gifts, provided her with a beautiful garden and built her a throne of her own, showing a different side to himself. Some say that

Persephone had softened her feelings towards him and eventually she started to fall in love with him, others say she did not as she had refused to eat during her stay there.

In the meantime her mother Demeter was grief stricken at the loss of her daughter, searching the earth over for her missing daughter. Finally, Hekate the goddess of magic and witchcraft told her that her daughter had been abducted but did not know by whom, they both approached Helios the god of the sun, who saw everything that happened on earth. He told her Hades had abducted her daughter.

Driven mad by her daughter's abduction Demeter had abandoned her duties, she threatened to make the earth barren destroying all of human-kind forever if her daughter was not returned to her. Zeus under pressure from Demeter and the other Gods who were annoyed by the cries and pleas of the suffering masses decided it was time to summon Hades informing him that Persephone must be returned to her mother.

Hades fearing losing Persephone forever had urged her to eat some pomegranate seeds before returning her aboveground, knowing that anyone who tastes the food of the underworld must remain in the underworld. Demeter became enraged upon hearing of Hades subterfuge, refusing to accept his pronouncement and so the two combatants engaged in a stand-off.

To resolve the dilemma Zeus ruled that Persephone would spend half the year with her mother Demeter above ground, restoring fertility with every visit and the other half of the year she would spend in underworld with her husband Hades.

Epilogue

"I am not what happened to me, I am what I choose to become" – Carl Gustav Jung

It is fourteen years on now and my children and I are living a life of our own choosing, it is filled with the many normal challenges that life presents, however it is markedly and blessedly free from the apprehension, suffering and oppression that was a malignant part of our past. My son and daughter are in their own respectively healthy and loving relationships, which brings me the greatest joy and contentment, reinforcing the belief that there can be true reconciliation, healing and redemption from past traumatic events. I have created a life that includes the peacefulness and the good kind of excitement that I dreamed of from the beginning, I have supportive and loving friends and family in my life to complete my happiness. I have finally come to peace with my past, resolving all the lingering disappointment, bitterness and resentment I was harbouring toward my ex-husband, my father and also toward myself. Upon reflection I truly believe that I was blessed twice during my past abusive relationship in the form of my two children and therefore could never view my previous circumstances with any regret. I see my children as gifts given in the face of adversity, they were my inspiration, giving me a reason to fight for a better life for them and for myself.

About five years after reuniting with my family my mother was diagnosed with leukemia and passed away shortly after, she was a strong woman who fought to the end but the disease got the better of her. I felt her loss deeply and I think of her every day, I have learned never to dwell on the wasted emotion of regret and so I never look back at the time we had lost during our separation. Instead, I focus on the precious time we had spent together before she passed away and will forever appreciate the love and joy she brought into my life and that of my children who grew to love her in the short time they had spent with her. I was blessed to have her as a mother, she was a kind, generous and loving person who possessed an indominable spirit, she taught me to be resourceful, creative and resilient and I am profoundly grateful for the time we shared together. I can feel her on my shoulder with every word I scribe, she is an inspiration for the books I have written and the ones I intend to write.

Just recently my ex-husband had passed away unexpectedly at the age of fifty-nine, he died of natural causes in his sleep. This came as a shock to us all and was especially distressing for my children who were very recently forging a more mature and positive relationship with their father. He was changing for the better toward them, spending time with them and taking more of an interest in their lives. On a personal level his demise had stunned me, I was confronted with a confusing mix of emotions, however I can absolutely remember being acutely aware of an overwhelming feeling of relief. It was as if a weight I did not realise I had been carrying had been lifted from me, an invisible chord had been severed freeing me from a bond that tied me to the past on some deeply inaccessible level, one that I was not consciously aware existed until this transpired. His passing, we were told was instantaneous, occurring while he was asleep indicating that he had not suffered or knew what was happening to him. For the next eight or so months that followed I could not shake the feeling of surreality about his death, in the sense that this larger-than-life figure who at one time was a monumentally terrifying influence in my life was no longer alive, it was hard to metabolise. I did not realise until he passed away that the effects of his abusive actions towards me which in the past were responsible for creating fundamental feelings of insecurity and fear, had remained lingering in the recesses of my psyche without my conscious awareness, despite the extensive work I had done to eradicate its' negative impact.

This was evidenced by the emotions I experienced post his passing which can only be described as a confusing mix of deeply profound feelings of true liberation, relief, and release coursing through my body as well as some unexpected residual sadness and grief over the loss of the possibility of what we could have had, had we both transcended the maladaptive beliefs and defences we had developed throughout our childhood. I was astounded that I was experiencing these unexpected feelings of release, I thought myself substantially free of the past and content with the life I had carved out for myself. My response to his death is significant and illustrates the length and depth of the impact that the abusive actions of one human-being can have on another and the fact that it can cast such a long shadow, leaving an enduring effect on the injured party's psyche. Uncannily on the night he passed away which was a Friday night and unbeknownst to me at the time was ironically the same night I was having a discussion with my closest girlfriends about whether or not I should assign a pseudonym to the first book I had written on the subject of abusers and their victims. I needed to make a decision as I was signing a contract with the publishers in a couple of days and was uncertain about how my ex-husband would react to the book should he find out about its existence and my friends were just as concerned. We were weighing up whether he would respond unfavourably and decided that he likely would, and so after much discussion I had reluctantly decided that I would assign a pseudonym to the book.

It was that same weekend that we were apprised of his passing, which was a strangely coincidental happening to say the least and of course consequently, I had decided to sign the book with my preferred name. It may seem like it has been a journey of epic proportions for me to get to this point in my life and looking back perhaps it was however, I never did take stock of the chronological time during my life as it served no purpose. Every victim of abuse will decide when the journey towards reclamation, redemption and wholeness will stop for them, as for me as I said before I will always be a work in progress and I am hoping that should I need to, I will continue to shed any unnecessary layers of superfluous psychological baggage that presents itself along the way. My express desire with this endeavour was to shed light on the origins and true nature of family and domestic abuse. Through highlighting the complexity of the underlying psychological and emotional issues that underpin abusive relationships and how it directs the course of both the victims and the abuser's lives. I hope that you the reader will come to appreciate that it is possible to alter the circumstances and trajectory of your life by taking a personal journey inward. It is only through one's conviction to commit to honest self-reflection, analysis, and review, combined with a willingness to accept new thoughts, concepts and beliefs that profound transformation can occur. Remember true and lasting change begins and ends within your own psyche, you are the captain of your destiny and only you can know what truly resides in your heart.

"Until you make the unconscious
conscious,
It will direct your life and you will call it fate"

Carl Gustav Jung

Carl Gustav Jung was a Swiss psychiatrist and philosopher, he is best known for his various works in psychology and widely considered to be the father of analytic psychology.

1875 – 1961

www.ingramcontent.com/pod-product-compliance
Lightning Source LLC
Chambersburg PA
CBHW060356290526
45791CB00002B/523